Enjoying American Wines

W9-CRN-632

JAY HARLOW
Writer

SUSAN LAMMERS
SALLY W. SMITH
Editors

LINDA HINRICHS
CAROL KRAMER
Designers

FRED LYON
Photographer

SANDRA LEARNED
Food Stylist

SARA SLAVIN
Photographic Stylist

Danielle Walker *(far left)* is chairman of the board and founder of the California Culinary Academy. **Jay Harlow** *(left)*, a free-lance cooking teacher and writer on food and wine, has been professionally involved with wine and food for over a decade. A graduate of Stanford University, he was formerly Administrative Director of the American Institute of Wine and Food. He has worked in the retail wine business and as a cook and chef at several fine restaurants in San Francisco and Berkeley, California, and is co-author of cookbooks on California seafood cookery and charcoal grilling.

The California Culinary Academy Among the forefront of American institutions leading the culinary renaissance in this country, the California Culinary Academy in San Francisco has gained a reputation as one of the most outstanding professional chef training schools in the world. With a teaching staff recruited from the best restaurants of Western Europe, the California Culinary Academy educates students from around the world in the preparation of classical cuisine. The recipes in this book were created in consultation with the chefs of the California Culinary Academy. For information about the Academy, write the Office of the Dean, California Culinary Academy, 625 Polk St., San Francisco, CA 94102.

Front Cover

The ideal place to enjoy wine is at the table. Pairing a fine, full-bodied Cabernet Sauvignon with roast lamb brings out the best in both—a good example of the art of matching food and wine. See "Wine & Food," pages 59–89, for a thorough discussion of how to combine wine and food, with many delicious recipes.

Title Page

An old stone winery building in California's Napa Valley provides the backdrop for a glass of Sauvignon Blanc, one of the fine wines of America.

Back Cover

Upper Left: Four Cornish game hens are arranged artfully on a platter with baby carrots and green beans. Among the lessons to be learned from professional chefs is that the way food is presented is just as important as how it tastes.

Upper Right: Veal Chops With Tarragon (see page 75)—the meat quickly sautéed, then topped with a deglazing sauce of tarragon-scented stock—are delicious with the subtle flavors of a California Pinot Noir.

Lower Left: The wines and foods typical of a region often complement each other. Here, a basket of New York State wines with apples and Cheddar from the same area.

Lower Right: Trout garnished with lemon and parsley are ready to enter the fish poacher, where they will be simmered in white wine and herbs.

Contributors

Calligrapher
Chuck Wertman

Illustrator
Ron Hildebrand

Additional Photographers
Michael Lamotte, back cover, upper left and lower right
Laurie Black, Academy photography
Fischella, photograph of Danielle Walker

Additional Food Stylists
Amy Nathan, back cover, upper left and lower right
Jeff Van Hanswyk, at The Academy

Editorial Staff
Teresa Castle
Catherine Pearsall
Rebecca Pepper

Art and Production Staff
Linda Bouchard
Deborah Cowder
Lezlly Freier
Kate O'Keeffe
Anne Pederson
Bill Yusavage

Lithographed in U.S.A. by
Webcrafters, Inc.

The California Culinary Academy series is produced by the staff of Ortho Information Services:

Publisher
Robert L. Iacopi

Production Director
Ernie S. Tasaki

Series Managing Editor
Sally W. Smith

Photographic Director
Alan Copeland

Address all inquiries to:
Ortho Information Services
Chevron Chemical Company
Consumer Products Division
575 Market Street
San Francisco, CA 94105

1 2 3 4 5 6 7 8 9
86 87 88 89 90 91

ISBN 0-89721-058-1

Library of Congress Catalog Card Number 85-073033

Chevron Chemical Company
575 Market Street, San Francisco, CA 94105

C O N T E N T S

Enjoying American Wines

The four-century tradition
of winemaking in North America
continues: Ripe grapes in
a California vineyard await
transformation into wine.

The Heritage of American Wine

Many Americans are just beginning to discover what the rest of the wine-growing world has known for centuries: that wine enhances the flavor of food and adds to the enjoyment of the dining experience. We are also learning that America can make wines to rank with the world's best. Come along on a tour of America's vineyards and wineries. Along the way you will learn how to select, store, serve, and cook with the remarkable wines of America, and most of all, how to match them with your favorite foods to add to your dining pleasure. First, a brief history of American wine.

THE NEW WORLD OF WINE

Wine is one of the oldest agricultural products. Like bread, another ancient food, it is more than a staple of everyday life; it is a symbol—of the harvest, of plenty, of hospitality, of celebration. From the beginnings of Western civilization, vineyards and wine have had important places in mythology, religion, medicine, and law. Records from Mesopotamia and Egypt show that viticulture (grape-growing), winemaking, and wine drinking were a part of human culture at least as far back as the third millennium B.C. Biblical references to wine go as far back as Genesis, in which Noah is depicted planting a vineyard and making wine. Many modern traditions involving wine, from toasting brides to christening ships, are directly descended from ancient ritual offerings to the gods.

Of course, most of us serve wine not for ritual purposes but as a simple matter of pleasure. Taken in moderation, it enhances the flavor of foods, aids digestion, provides a mild stimulation of the senses, promotes good health (see "Wine and Health," page 7), and contributes to the enjoyment of the daily process of eating. In short, it is part of "the good life."

Wine is meant to be enjoyed. Yet somehow it has developed a mystique that some people find intimidating. There is a common belief that one has to be an "expert" or "connoisseur" to appreciate wine, but this is not true at all. You are your own expert, the ultimate authority on your own taste in wine and food. Let your taste be your guide, even in approaching the recommendations of particular wines, and wine and food combinations, in this book.

What exactly is wine? As it is generally understood (and even legally defined in many countries), wine is the fermented juice of sound, ripe grapes. To the chemist, it is a complex liquid containing water, ethanol (ethyl alcohol), organic acids, proteins, vitamins, minerals, esters, and sugars. To some religious groups it is a sacrament, while to others it is forbidden. To governments, it is variously known as a substance to be regulated and taxed; an important trade commodity; a source of local, regional, or national pride; and a foodstuff to be inspected. To most residents of the wine-growing regions of the world, it is a staple, like bread. And to those who appreciate good food, it is an enjoyable part of everyday dining and special meals.

American wine is nothing new. Wine has been made on this continent since the first European settlers arrived in the sixteenth century. But only in this century has wine become a part of mainstream American culture. Today, a growing number of Americans drink wine, not just on special occasions, but with everyday meals and at informal gatherings. We are developing a culture that takes an avid interest in wine and appreciates the pleasures and tastes it offers.

The United States now ranks sixth in the world in the total volume of wine produced. However, we have one of the lowest rates of wine consumption per capita (2.25 gallons, or about 12 bottles, per capita in 1982, versus 22.7 gallons in France, which leads all nations in the consumption of wine). Until recently, wine consumption in America was limited to just a small part of the population. One segment was recent immigrants, or their offspring, from the wine-growing regions of Europe, who maintained European preferences for food and wine. Relatively wealthy, well-traveled Americans also brought home the tradition of drinking wine with meals, as did American servicemen who returned from overseas after both world wars. But apart from these relative few, wine as an everyday part of dining remained outside the American mainstream; the majority of American wines were of the high-alcohol "fortified" or "dessert" type—port, sherry, muscatel, and the like.

By the late 1960s, however, table wine (unflavored and unfortified wine under 14 percent alcohol) began to outsell the fortified variety. The trend has continued, and even accelerated. In 1983, 76.4 percent of the wine sold in this country was table wine, and of the remainder a considerable amount was sparkling wine. In the same year, our national consumption of wine surpassed that of distilled spirits for the first time. We still drink far less wine than most Europeans, but we are coming to resemble them more and more in the types of wine we drink.

A BRIEF HISTORY OF THE VINE AND WINEMAKING IN AMERICA

Just as wine begins as grapes, so a history of American wine must begin with a discussion of grapes. Early Norse explorers of North America found such a profusion of wild grape vines that they called this continent Vinland. Indeed, this continent is home to over a dozen species of the genus *Vitis,* many of which provide edible grapes. In the sixteenth century, as settlers from Europe began arriving in larger numbers, they were delighted to find wild grapes growing all along the Atlantic coast, and promptly set out to make wine. Unfortunately, the native vines (chiefly *V. labrusca* in the Northeast and *V. rotundifolia* farther south) made wines that tasted strange to their palates, accustomed as they were to European wines.

The next step seemed sensible enough: If the native grapes did not make good wine, why not grow the varieties that made the wine they remembered from home? As a result, cuttings of choice varieties were brought from Europe and widely planted in the colonies. Unfortunately, the pioneers had no way of knowing that a combination of climate and a host of fungus and viruslike diseases endemic to this continent would foil their plans.

VINIFERA IN THE EAST: EARLY ATTEMPTS

The Eurasian vine *Vitis vinifera*—the species that produces all the famous wines of Europe—grows in a wide range of climate zones, from the Mediterranean coast of North Africa to northern France and Germany. Most of these areas, however, share two important qualities: relatively mild winters and rather dry summers. Some areas of North America were simply too cold in winter for vinifera vines. Another problem was our summer rains, which promoted fungus diseases such as powdery mildew. American soils also harbored a root-damaging insect called phylloxera. Native grape species had long since developed resistance to these pests, as well as winter hardiness, but time and again, the American environment proved too hostile for the European transplants. Still, the settlers in what would become the eastern United States felt sure that some grapes would thrive in their new home, so they turned their attention to finding and cultivating the best varieties of the native labrusca grapes.

Because grapes offer a wide range of varieties within each species and readily form hybrids, the settlers had a considerable array of material to work with. Some varieties, when made into wine, showed less of the "foxy" aroma typical of labrusca. (The aroma and flavor term *foxy* comes from the common name of the species, the fox grape, rather than from any perceived resemblance to foxes.) Because the pioneer American viticulturalists seldom kept records, it is impossible to trace the origin of the earliest varieties they developed, but it seems likely that some of them have elements of *V. vinifera* in their ancestry. These chance crosses of the American and Eurasian vines anticipated the French-American hybrids that became an important part of the eastern U.S. wine industry a few centuries later.

VINIFERA IN THE WEST

Meanwhile, at the other end of the continent, the seeds of the California wine industry were literally being sown. In the sixteenth century, Spanish missionaries to the New World began to plant vinifera grapes for the purpose of making altar wines. The most successful variety, known as Criolla (Spanish for "Creole"), was apparently brought to Mexico as a seed rather than as a cutting. Because vines grown from seed (as opposed to cuttings) do not always exhibit the same qualities as their parents, it is impossible to trace this grape to any European ancestor, although it presumably came from Spain. Whatever its heritage, the white grape bore fruit in Mexico, achieving its purpose of providing the Catholic missionaries with wine for the Mass. The grape was particularly successful in Baja California, where it produced enough wine to export to other parts of the Spanish colonies. The Eurasian vine had finally found a home in North America.

As the Franciscan friars moved northward into what would become California, establishing the famous series of missions from San Diego (in 1769) to Sonoma (1823), they brought with them a need for altar wine. Soon after the missions were established, they sent for cuttings of the reliable Criolla grape. (There is a romantic popular notion of Father Junipero Serra—founder of many of the missions—carrying the vine with him as he went north and personally planting the first vineyards, but it has no basis in fact.) By the 1830s, there were quite a few acres of secular vineyards as well, based on the same adaptable but unremarkable variety, which became known in English as the Mission grape.

WINE AND HEALTH

Wine is an extremely complex beverage. Some of the nutritional qualities of the fresh grape remain in wine, while others are transformed by the fermentation process. Wine has been shown to contain vitamins A and C, various B vitamins, and all essential dietary minerals in measurable amounts. The small amounts of nonfermenting grape sugars that remain in wine are easily assimilated by the body as a source of caloric energy.

Moderation is the key to the beneficial effects of wine. In modest amounts, the alcohol in wine acts as a relaxant but in larger doses it dulls the senses and inhibits the overall functioning of the nervous system. A relatively low concentration of alcohol (such as that in wine) stimulates the appetite and the flow of digestive juices, but the high concentration of alcohol in distilled spirits depresses these same functions.

There is a growing body of medical knowledge that shows that regular, moderate intake of alcohol is actually beneficial to health. A large-scale study in California showed that moderate drinkers have a lower risk of heart attack than either heavy drinkers or nondrinkers, and that moderate alcohol consumption does not increase blood pressure, as heavy consumption does.

Two Viticultural Pioneers

The California wine story for the next three decades is dominated by two Europeans who saw the potential in the state's Mediterranean-style climate. A Frenchman, appropriately named Jean-Louis Vignes (French for "vines"), had choice varieties shipped from France beginning in 1834 and planted them near Los Angeles. Others followed his example, and vinifera varieties spread rapidly throughout the state. The California wine industry was already well under way by the Gold Rush of 1849.

The contribution of Vignes, in reputation if not entirely in fact, was overshadowed by that of Agoston Haraszthy, who in 1861 shipped from Europe thousands of cuttings of over 300 grape varieties. "Count" Haraszthy (actually a minor member of the Hungarian nobility, he later went by the no more accurate title of "Colonel") eventually founded the Buena Vista winery, which is still in existence. The flamboyant Haraszthy's almost legendary role and title of "the father of modern California viticulture" obscures the contributions of many other pioneers, but he is a symbol of the explosion of the California wine industry in the mid-nineteenth century. As early as 1856, California wines were being exported to Europe, South America, and Asia; in 1900, 28 California wineries received medals or honorable mention at the Paris Exposition.

While California was building its business based on the vinifera grape, winemakers in the east were developing more and better varieties from crosses of native grapes. One, the familiar blue-black Concord, became so popular for its adaptability, hardiness, and productivity that it quickly became dominant east of the Rockies. Other varieties developed in the mid-nineteenth century (and still important today) included the Catawba, Delaware, Isabella, and Niagara. These, too, produced award-winning wines at the Paris Exposition of 1900.

PHYLLOXERA AND PROHIBITION

America's other "gifts" to the nineteenth-century world of wine were less welcome. Vine cuttings shipped back and forth across the Atlantic during the early nineteenth century had carried with them several fungus diseases, notably powdery mildew and black rot. These diseases, against which the European vines had no resistance, caused widespread damage in the Old World vineyards. Eventually they were controlled, at least to the level of a predictable nuisance. But another hitchhiking American pest, the vine louse phylloxera, arrived in France in 1863 and changed European winemaking forever. Vast areas, including the most famous vineyards in the world, were devastated by the root-damaging insect. The solution, like the scourge, came from America: Since the pest was endemic in this country, the widespread and prolific American vines must have been immune to its effects. By grafting bud wood of the European vines onto American rootstocks, the vineyards (perhaps even the noblest varieties of Europe) were saved. Yet the debate goes on, among those fortunate enough to taste the wines of "pre-phylloxera" vines, whether the modern wines will ever be as good.

Phylloxera appeared in California, where it did not naturally occur, in 1873 and wreaked similar havoc on the state's vineyards before it was checked, also by grafting onto the rootstocks of native American varieties. An interesting experiment on the "prephylloxera" question is now being carried out in some of the large new plantings in the Central Coast counties of California; since these areas were never planted with vines during the phylloxera era, vineyardists in search of more varietal character are gambling on planting ungrafted vine cuttings (that is, without the protection of phylloxera-resistant rootstocks)—and watching carefully for any sign of the pest.

Phylloxera was stopped before it destroyed the California wine industry. But another, even more disruptive, danger lay ahead: Prohibition.

The "temperance" movement was originally a noble cause, a campaign against the dangers of excessive use of alcohol. In its original sense, "moderation and self-restraint," temperance was entirely consistent with the use of table wine. In fact, many advocates of American wine, from Thomas Jefferson forward, stressed the positive value of wine as an alternative to distilled spirits. But by the end of the nineteenth century, the temperance movement drew no distinction between wine and spirits. Beginning in the 1880s, cities, counties, and whole states gradually "voted dry," that is, prohibited alcoholic beverages in any form. The movement finally led to the nationwide Prohibition of 1920 to 1933.

The Eighteenth Amendment and the Volstead Act (1920), which were the fruit of the Prohibition movement, made illegal "the manufacture, sale, or transportation of intoxicating liquors . . . for beverage purposes" throughout the United States. There were a few exceptions: wines for religious purposes were exempt, as were medicinal preparations based upon wine and available by prescription. But by and large, Prohibition crippled the American wine industry.

Of course, the law did not prevent people who wanted to drink from doing so; it just made it more difficult. The most dramatic effect of Prohibition was the widespread lawlessness of the Roaring Twenties, of which speakeasies and bathtub gin were only the colorful surface.

Before long, someone discovered a loophole of sorts in the Volstead Act: a section that allowed a head of household to make up to 200 gallons a year of "nonintoxicating cider and fruit juices" for home use. Now, enough people knew that grape juice

Although the American wine industry is comparatively young, it has produced some truly world-class wines, such as these Napa Valley Cabernets.

Zinfandel is one of dozens of varieties of Vitis vinifera, the Eurasian vine species that produces the finest wines in America, as well as in Europe.

plus yeast equals wine to create a home winemaking boom. While by no means legal, this practice became widespread enough that it created a whole new market for wine grapes. From 1920 to 1925, tons of California wine grapes were shipped by rail to amateur winemakers in eastern cities, who apparently preferred vinifera grapes to the local varieties.

Unfortunately, the home-wine market was less concerned with the flavor of the grapes than with how well they could be shipped to distant markets. To ensure that their grapes would arrive intact, many California growers grafted their vines to heavy-bearing, thick-skinned varieties; these grapes shipped well, but they made mediocre wine. By 1925, the market was saturated, and a grape glut developed. With no market for their grapes, many growers simply abandoned their vineyards.

REPEAL AND RECOVERY

By the time Prohibition was repealed in 1933, the wine industry was in a shambles. Some wineries had kept their doors open by making altar wines, but many more had been neglected. The first year or two after Repeal saw a lot of poorly made wine rushed to a thirsty market before it was ready to drink. But a conscientious effort to rebuild the American wine industry was under way, and in a few short years excellent wines were again being made.

The late 1930s saw two major developments that would have profound effects: the increase in "varietal" labeling, especially in California wines, and the introduction of French-American hybrid grapes in the eastern states.

Varietal Labeling

During the first century of the California wine industry, winemakers freely borrowed the names of European wines and regions to label their products, rather than giving them varietal names (names based on the variety of grape from which they were made). There were certainly exceptions; many early American-made wines were labeled by variety, such as Zinfandel, Cabernet Sauvignon, or Riesling. But the more common practice was to use names such as burgundy, Chablis, Rhine, claret, or Champagne—names based on a European wine or a wine-growing region. This sort of imitation irritated the wine growers of Europe, who argued (rightly) that these names had very specific meanings in terms of local origin, grape types, and vineyard and wine cellar practices. But in America, if a winemaker thought his red wine tasted like the red wine of Burgundy, France, it seemed perfectly reasonable to call it Smith's California Burgundy or Chateau Smith Burgundy. Thus a number of names with very specific meanings in Europe became the "generic" names that persist to this day in the United States.

In the late 1930s, however, a wine-importing American named Frank Schoonmaker put his foot down, refusing to carry in his line any California wines with European names. Instead, he insisted that they be labeled according to the type of grape from which they were made. If a wine was made from Chardonnay, the grape used to make the great French white Burgundies (including Chablis), then rather than calling it California Chablis, he said, call it California Chardonnay.

The trend toward such "varietal" labeling took hold as consumers began to taste the difference between, say, a fine Cabernet Sauvignon and a claret made of any red grapes that were available. The higher prices that the better varietals brought to the vintner caused a long-term shift in the pattern of vineyard planting, and fine varietals have dominated new vineyard plantings ever since.

The Hybrid Revolution in the East

Around the same time as Schoonmaker was promoting varietal labeling, another American was advocating a whole new range of varieties to growers in the eastern United States. Philip Wagner, a journalist and amateur winemaker, began importing a number of French-American hybrids from France and planting them in his Maryland vineyard. These hybrids, developed in France as a by-product of the fight against phylloxera, combined the winter hardiness and disease resistance of their American parents with a flavor much more like European grapes. Now, argued Wagner, it was possible in the eastern states to make wines without the "foxy" flavor of native grapes. Wagner has been an advocate of hybrid grapes and their wines ever since, demonstrating their potential at his Boordy Vineyards winery in Maryland before "retiring" in the 1970s to the vine nursery business.

While labrusca grapes are still widely popular in most states east of the Rockies, the hybrids are becoming increasingly important. Many of the major established eastern wineries are incorporating more hybrid grapes in their wines, and a majority of the new wineries are solely devoted to hybrid and vinifera grapes.

Despite the troubled history of vinifera in the East, a dedicated minority continues to grow this species in selected areas. So far the results are encouraging. The modern pioneer is Dr. Konstantin Frank, who decided in the 1950s that if hybrids could grow in the Finger Lakes region of upstate New York, so could the hardier vinifera varieties. The winery he founded, now known as Vinifera Wine Cellars, has proven the point to the satisfaction of many, producing highly regarded Chardonnay and Riesling, among other types of wine. A hardy and expanding band of growers and winemakers is exploring other areas around the country where vinifera vines will bear fruit, and the years ahead will undoubtedly see more wines of this type from locations once thought to be too cold, too warm, too dry, or too rainy for this species.

AMERICA: ONE HUGE VINEYARD

Wine growing in the West long ago expanded beyond California. The Pacific Northwest includes vineyard areas as disparate as the cool, moist valleys of western Oregon and the semiarid interior of Washington and western Idaho. Arizona and New Mexico both have small industries based on vinifera, and Texas is on the verge of being an important wine state. The years to come will undoubtedly produce more American wines, as growers and winemakers expand into new areas or revive old vineyard districts, as well as better wines as vintners discover the best varieties and winemaking techniques for each area.

Along with an increase in the variety and quality of American wine will come a natural increase in the number of American wine drinkers. If present trends continue, we as a nation will consume more and more wine per person, and more of it will be table wine. Before too long, a bottle of wine on the dinner table will be as commonplace a sight in the average American home as it is in France, Italy, or any other major wine-growing nation.

Promise of things to come: Sprouting vines in a California vineyard, the first step in the process that culminates in bottled wine.

From the Vine to the Bottle

VINEYARDS

The wine in your glass is a product of nature, guided from time to time by the human hand. Wine is not really made so much as it is allowed to happen. A skillful winemaker can direct the winemaking process to bring out the best qualities of a batch of grapes, but the quality itself comes from the vine, the soil, and the weather, as the water and minerals of the soil and the energy of the sun are transformed into ripe, sweet grapes. In the pages that follow, that process is explained.

HOW WINE IS MADE

To understand how wine is made and what distinguishes a great wine from an ordinary one, we must begin in the vineyard. It is here that the vine transforms the water and minerals of the soil and the energy of the sun into ripe, sweet grapes.

Wine grapes will grow almost anywhere in North America where winters are not too severe. This excludes Alaska and most of Canada, the northern Great Plains states, and the higher altitudes of the Rocky Mountains. However, there are favored locations for the vine as far north as British Columbia, the Great Lakes region, and southern New England. Most of these are near large bodies of water, which moderate winter temperatures, and they tend to be on the sunniest south- or west-facing slopes. At the southern end of the range, all but the coolest microclimates (usually found near water or at high altitudes) are too warm to produce high-quality grapes. Each variety of grape requires a certain range of conditions to produce the best fruit, which will, in turn, make the best wine. The first step in producing a good wine is to plant a grape variety suited to the local growing conditions.

The most important factor in the choice of a grape for a particular location is climate. Some varieties can tolerate more winter cold than others, some more summer rain. Some varieties ripen earlier than others, making them desirable for areas with short growing seasons. Varieties that form buds early are likely to be damaged by spring frosts, which are a common occurrence in some vineyard areas. Summer temperatures are especially important to the flavor of each variety. Many areas that produce first-rate Zinfandel, for example, are too warm to produce great Riesling; conversely, Zinfandel will not always ripen fully in a cooler district that produces fine Rieslings.

Another important factor to consider in choosing a grape for a particular site is the soil. Unlike most crops, which require rich, fertile soil, some grapes actually make better wines if grown in poor, rocky soil. Some of the best California Pinot Noir is grown on shallow soil overlying limestone, and Cabernet Sauvignons made from grapes grown in volcanic soil in the hills alongside the Napa Valley have a distinctive flavor.

Economics and changing fashions in wine play a part in planting decisions, too. In the 1960s and 1970s, as the demand for California Cabernet wines increased, so did the price of Cabernet grapes, and plantings of this variety soared. By the time these vines were mature, white wines were more popular, and the rush was on to plant Chardonnay.

Through the decades, a combination of careful experimentation and trial and error have shown which varieties will grow and ripen in each vineyard area. Growers and winemakers are now turning their attention to learning which variety produces the *best* possible wine in each area, and gradually converting vineyards of less desirable varieties to the best types for the location. This process has been going on for centuries in Europe, with the result that all the great white wines of the Burgundy region are made from Chardonnay grapes, while those of Bordeaux are made from Sauvignon Blanc and Semillon, and in the great German vineyards of the Rhine and Mosel, the choice variety is Riesling. In the decades to come, American wines should show more and more of this kind of regional and local specialization. The part of the Napa Valley around Rutherford is now planted almost exclusively with Cabernet and related varieties, while a few miles south in the Carneros district, Pinot Noir and Chardonnay dominate. The result of this kind of specialization—happily for American wine drinkers—should be better and better wines.

THE VINEYARD

Once the grower has decided which varieties to plant, a process is begun that will take several years to, literally, bear fruit. After clearing and plowing the land, the grower lays out the vineyard in rows, by driving stakes at carefully measured distances in each row and planting a young nursery-raised vine next to each stake. In most vinifera vineyards (see page 7), cuttings of the desired variety are grafted onto rootstocks of native American varieties resistant to the soil pest phylloxera (see page 8).

Over the next three years, the vine must be carefully pruned and trained. Left on its own, the vine would sprawl on the ground in every direction, producing plenty of greenery and lots of small, inconsequential grapes. To get the best fruit, and to make harvesting easier, the grower carefully controls the size and shape of the vine. By training the vine first to the stake, then to horizontal wires strung between the stakes, the grower gradually forms the vine into a shape that resembles a small, T-shaped tree 3 to 5 feet tall. In the third or fourth year, the arms of the vine sprout the new fruit-bearing wood that will produce the year's crop.

With care, the vine will produce grapes for half a century or more. The art of the grower is to understand and work with the vine, guiding and pruning to balance the needs of the vine and the needs of the winemaker. If pruned too severely, the vine will have to put all of its energy into growing leaves to sustain itself. If the vine is allowed to overgrow, it will produce abundant fruit, but the flavor of the grapes will be diminished. When all is in balance, the leaves produce plenty of sugar, which is stored in a limited number of clusters of ripe, sweet, juicy grapes full of the particular flavor of the variety and the subtle flavors imparted by the minerals in the local soil and water.

The Annual Cycle of the Vine

The grapevine is a deciduous plant; it loses its leaves in autumn and becomes dormant in the winter. A mature vineyard in winter looks like a miniature orchard of gnarled, leafless trees standing in stark contrast to wild grasses and weeds or to snow. By the first day of spring, however, green buds begin to swell and open. These quickly turn into leafy shoots, with tendrils looking for a surface on which to climb.

Later in the spring, when the vine is in full leaf, clusters of flower buds, looking like tiny green grapes, appear. At this point growers and winemakers watch the weather nervously, because a bad frost can kill the flowers and wipe out most of the year's crop. This is a serious danger in many vineyards, especially those located on valley floors, where the coldest air settles on frosty nights. Growers have several ways to protect the vines from these late spring frosts. The traditional smudgepots, which were kept burning all night in the vineyards when frost danger was highest, have mostly given way to large fans or sprinklers. The fans circulate the air, keeping the coldest pockets of air from settling in any one spot. The sprinklers, surprisingly, use ice to protect the buds from frost: As the temperature drops, the water forms a thin layer of ice on the buds, effectively insulating them from any further drop in temperature. The buds can survive this 32° F chill, but temperatures a few degrees lower would be fatal.

If the buds escape a killing frost, they may still face the danger of heavy rains, which prevent pollination of the flowers. However, if the weather cooperates, the flowers will set fruit by the end of the spring. Through the summer, photosynthesis in the leaves of the vine combines energy from sunlight, carbon dioxide from the air, and water from the soil to form the sugar that feeds the plant.

By late summer, the grapes begin to swell with water and sugar, and the skins change from green to red, blue-black, yellow, or purple, depending on the variety.

The grower has many decisions to make during the ripening season. If the vineyard is in a dry area, it may be necessary to irrigate the vines. Watering too heavily or too near the harvest date, however, can swell the grapes, producing a thin, watery wine. The grower may choose to thin the crop at some stage, removing up to half of the immature grape bunches to concentrate the flavor in the remaining fruit. As harvest time approaches, some of the excess leaf growth is removed to allow access to the grapes, but enough must be left to shade the grapes from the sun and provide a steady supply of sugar.

The most crucial decision is when to harvest. The grower and winemaker (sometimes the same person) carefully check the grapes each day, always keeping an eye on the sky for signs of rain. A small sample of juice is analyzed in the lab for sugar and acid content and tasted for the more intangible flavor components. Each day, if the sun shines, the grapes become a little sweeter and a little less acid. Up to a point, more ripeness means better wine; the extra sugar will turn into a higher degree of alcohol, giving the wine more body and more aging potential. But if the grapes get too ripe, they develop a raisiny flavor that carries over to the wine. The worst thing that can happen at this point is a heavy rain; first the vine soaks up a lot of water, swelling the grapes and reducing the concentration of sugar, then mold and mildew settle on the wet grapes, spoiling the flavor.

When the decision to pick is made, the picking crews work hard and fast to bring the crop in quickly. Grapes are traditionally harvested by hand in a process that has changed little in thousands of years. Many newer vineyards, however, have been planted with wider rows and taller vines to allow mechanical harvesting. Some growers and winemakers swear by this method because it saves on labor costs and brings in the crop very quickly, before the condition of the grapes can change. Others prefer the human touch and the trained eye, which may pass over a bunch of grapes that is underripe or overripe. Both systems are here to stay, and the debate will go on forever.

After the harvest, most of the activity shifts indoors to the winery, but there is still work to be done in the vineyard. In cold-winter areas, soil may have to be piled up around the trunk of the vine to protect it from freezing. When the vine is completely dormant, it is time to prune. Most of the year's new wood is removed, leaving behind only the older wood and the "canes" that will provide next year's fruit. The vine rests until spring, when the cycle begins again.

*Against a background of
Semillon grapes, four views of
a vineyard through the seasons—
a timeless cycle of new growth,
harvest, dormancy, and renewal.*

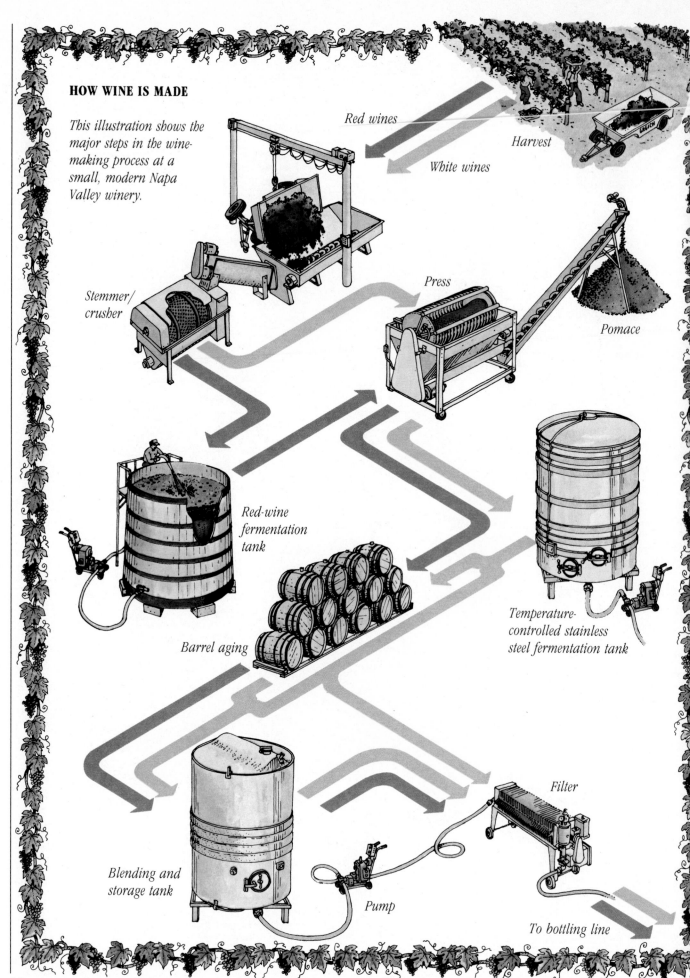

HOW WINE IS MADE

This illustration shows the major steps in the wine-making process at a small, modern Napa Valley winery.

Harvest

Red wines

White wines

Stemmer/crusher

Press

Pomace

Red-wine fermentation tank

Temperature-controlled stainless steel fermentation tank

Barrel aging

Blending and storage tank

Pump

Filter

To bottling line

THE WINEMAKING PROCESS

Somewhere in the early history of agriculture, someone discovered that if you crush some grapes, squeeze out the juice, and let it stand for a while, you will have a tasty, mildly intoxicating beverage. Left too long, however, it became disagreeably sour. Gradually our ancestors learned to control the process to make a wine that would last (at least until the next vintage). The art and science of winemaking has advanced considerably since then, but we are still dealing with a simple, natural process. By intervening at several points along the way, however, the winemaker can have a considerable influence on the final product.

From the moment the grapes arrive at the winery, the actions and decisions of the winemaker determine to a large extent what kind of wine will result—whether it will be sweet or dry, red, white, or rosé, still or sparkling. Modern machinery has taken the place of much of the traditional equipment of the winemaker, but the modern process is just a refinement of the techniques practiced by all winemakers throughout history.

The first step is to crush the grapes and remove them from the stems. Traditionally this was done by treading on the grapes in open troughs. In modern wineries, the grapes are crushed by a machine that also separates the fruit from the stems. What happens after crushing determines the color and, of course, the flavor of the finished wine.

For red wine, the grapes go from the crusher—seeds, skins, and all (but minus the stems)—into the fermenting vat. The *must*, or unfermented juice, ferments in contact with the skins for a period of a few days to two weeks or more. During this time, the must absorbs pigments from the skins, giving the wine a deep, purplish red color. As the must ferments, the skins and seeds float to the top, forming a thick "cap" that must be frequently mixed back into the wine, either by "punching down" (breaking up the cap with a wooden paddle and pushing the chunks of skins and seeds back down into the wine) or by pumping the wine from the bottom of the tank over the cap. After the wine has achieved the desired amount of fermentation "on the skins," it is pressed, and the skins and seeds are removed. The longer the wine ferments on the skins, the more color and tannin it extracts from them. The decision of when to press, then, depends on the type of wine desired. Cabernet and Merlot are typically kept on the skins for up to two weeks, regardless of how long it takes to convert all the sugar. Red wines made in a lighter, less tannic style are pressed sooner—as soon as three or four days in the case of some Gamays—and complete their fermentation in tanks or barrels.

For white wines, the grapes go directly from the crusher to the press. The traditional wooden basket press, so widely used that it has become a symbol of the winemaking process, is giving way to stainless steel presses, but the function is the same: to squeeze the juice out of the grapes, leaving behind the skins, seeds, and some of the grape pulp. Care must be taken not to press the grapes too hard, or the seeds will be crushed, giving the wine a bitter, harsh flavor. Once all the juice is squeezed out of the grapes, the press *pomace* (the skins and seeds) is returned to the vineyard to fertilize the soil.

Rosé wines are made by an intermediate process, fermenting in contact with the skins for only a day or two before pressing, then continuing to ferment like a white wine. Wines of a relatively new category, *blanc de noirs*, are made from red grapes pressed immediately and fermented as white wines (see "White Wine From Red Grapes?" at right).

WHITE WINE FROM RED GRAPES?

Since the late 1970s, the demand for white wines has risen much faster than the demand for red. As a result, many wineries in California have found themselves with a surplus of red grapes and red wines.

Of course, the color of red grapes is mainly in the skins; by pressing the grapes right away, you can produce a light-colored juice. French Champagne has traditionally been made with a third or more Pinot Noir, a dark-skinned grape. Some areas of Europe produce blanc de noirs, white wines made from "black" grapes. The Californians reasoned: Why not try the same technique here?

Thus, out of economic necessity, a new type of table wine has come on the market, as one winery after another has jumped on the blanc de noirs bandwagon. And these wines have become very popular. Most have some pinkish color, from a pale coppery hue to a bright salmon pink that could just as easily be called a rosé. They are especially pretty outdoors, and their flavors—a bit fuller than most whites, but without the harshness of younger reds—seem at their best with alfresco meals.

While this new genre now seems well established, there is still no universally accepted name for the type. Blanc de noirs is difficult to pronounce; oeil de perdrix (eye of the partridge), the French term for the color, is even more intimidating. A few wineries use the term vin gris *(gray wine), a name for similarly colored wines in France. But many more wineries are using names like White Zinfandel, Pinot Noir Blanc, or their own proprietary names. One winery, Weibel, refers to its selection of these wines as* blush varietals, *a term that just might catch on.*

Ripe grapes, such as those shown here entering a stemmer/crusher, can contain as much as 25 percent sugar by weight, making them among the sweetest fruits grown by man. Fermentation by microscopic yeast cells turns the sugar to alcohol, and the juice into wine.

Yeast and Fermentation

A modern winery is able to make a whole range of wines, from table wines and sparkling wines to the higher-alcohol port and sherry types. The basis of all of these wines is the fermentation of the grape juice by a single-celled organism, the wine yeast *Saccharomyces cereviseae.* The yeast feeds on the sugars in fresh fruits, such as grapes, and produces ethyl alcohol (ethanol) and carbon dioxide gas as by-products. Fermentation was a natural part of the life cycle of grapes long before anyone learned to make wine. In fact, the role of yeast in fermentation was only discovered a little over a century ago, by Louis Pasteur. Yeast cells are naturally present on the skins of grapes, so the simple act of crushing grapes inocu-

lates the must with yeast cells. These "wild" yeasts produce inconsistent fermentation, however. Most wine-makers use sulfur dioxide at the time of crushing to kill most of the wild yeasts, then add a "pure" strain of cultured yeast with known properties.

Once the yeast starter is added to the grapes (or juice) in the fermenting vessel, the yeast quickly multiplies, and before long millions of yeast cells are alive in the must. For several days, the must ferments rapidly, and the carbon dioxide quickly bubbles out of the fermenting tank. Gradually, as the sugar is consumed and the alcohol level rises, the yeast cells begin to die and settle to the bottom of the tank.

Left alone, the wine will ferment completely dry, that is, until there is no sugar remaining. However, the winemaker can control the fermentation process to achieve the desired result in several ways: temperature control, introduction of sulfur dioxide, and filtration.

Temperature control is important for some wines, especially the lighter, more delicate whites. During fermentation, the activity of the yeast cells creates heat in the wine. Uncontrolled, the temperature in the fermenting tank may reach 90° F. At this temperature, some of the fresh-fruit aromas would be lost through chemical changes. If the temperature is kept lower, the resulting wine has more of the aroma of the fresh grape. To preserve this fruity character, many wineries now ferment their white wines in stainless steel tanks jacketed with refrigeration coils.

Temperature control is not as important for the fermentation of red wine. In fact, many wineries believe that letting certain red wines, particularly Pinot Noir, get quite warm during fermentation actually helps the wine develop more flavor. In many cases, just keeping the winery air temperature down will prevent the red wines from getting too hot.

The natural tendency of wine is to ferment until it is completely dry. However, many wines are intentionally bottled with some residual sugar. In order to prevent sweet wines from continuing to ferment in the bottle (which causes fizzy wines or even exploding bottles), the winemaker must remove all traces of live yeast from the wine. One way to do this is with a fairly strong dose of sulfur dioxide, the workhorse sterilizing agent of the winemaking process. However, because too much sulfur dioxide is noticeable in the finished wine, it must be added in carefully measured doses.

Another technique for producing sweet wines is *sterile filtration*. The first step in this process is usually to chill the wine to near freezing. At this temperature, most of the yeast becomes dormant and sinks to the bottom. The wine is siphoned off and put through several stages of filters, the last of which is so fine that it filters out any remaining yeast cells. The wine can then be safely bottled with no fear of refermentation.

A third method of making a sweet wine is to let the wine ferment dry, then add a small amount of reserved, unfermented juice. By a combination of chilling, sulfur dioxide, and sterile filtration, the sweet juice can be kept from fermenting until the wine is ready for final blending. Because the blend is assembled according to taste, this method gives the most precise control over the sweetness of the finished wine.

Aging the Wine

After fermentation is complete, the winemaker faces another set of decisions. The first is whether or not to age the wine. Some white wines are at their best soon after fermentation is complete, when the flavor and aroma are freshest. But some of the fuller-bodied whites, especially Chardonnay, become more complex, satisfying wines when aged at least a few months in oak barrels. Barrel aging is standard for most red wines, because it mellows the harsh flavors of the young wine.

Experts disagree on exactly what chemical reactions occur inside the barrel, and particularly on the role of oxygen. But most wine lovers agree on the benefits of aging wine, especially red wine, in barrels: it softens the tannin and acids, producing a smoother wine, and develops small quantities of esters, aldehydes, and other organic compounds that add more complex flavors and "bouquet."

Most red wines, and some whites, are aged in small oak barrels before bottling. This aging produces a smoother, more complex, "rounder" flavor. Barrel sizes vary, but the size shown here (about 60 gallons capacity) is typical. Each barrel holds the equivalent of 25 cases of finished wine.

Even the type of wood used to make the barrels can affect the flavor of the wine. Oak is the traditional favorite, but oak from different sources can give different results. Many American wines are aged in barrels made of French oak, in an attempt to get a flavor more like that of French wines. Even among French oaks, some winemakers prefer the oak from the Limousin forest, others the oak of Nevers or Allier. American and Yugoslavian oak are also widely used, and each variety has its advocates. Many older California wineries age red wines in large tanks of redwood, which adds no flavor of its own, but allows natural aging reactions to occur.

Of course, barrel aging, like any good thing, can be overdone. New oak has a tendency to give a strong woody flavor to the wine and to contribute tannin of its own, so it must be used carefully. Aging too long in the barrel can produce a tired-tasting wine with little fruit. Once again, the nose and palate of a skilled winemaker are essential to get the best results from the aging process.

Some wines undergo a second type of fermentation, known as *malolactic fermentation*, after the sugar fermentation is complete. Malolactic bacteria transform one of the natural grape acids, malic acid, into the less-tart-tasting lactic acid. This normally occurs in the barrel, and the small amount of gas produced evaporates. Sometimes, however, it occurs in a bottled wine, making the wine slightly or unpleasantly gassy. However, with careful winemaking, this problem is rare.

Clarifying: Fining and Filtering

When the newly fermented wine is put into barrels, it is cloudy with suspended grape proteins and yeast cells. As it sits, these impurities usually settle to the bottom. Careful *racking*, or siphoning, of the wine off these *lees*, or sediments, gives a clear wine. But if cloudiness remains, or if the winemaker wants an exceptionally clear wine, he may *filter* or *fine* the wine. Fining is a traditional method: a fining agent such as egg whites, isinglass, or bentonite is poured over the surface of the wine, and as it slowly sinks through the wine, it attracts suspended molecules and carries them to the bottom. Filtering is a more modern process: The wine is filtered under pressure and spun at high speed in a centrifuge, which forces the heavier particles to the bottom in a speeded-up version of the natural settling process.

All of these ways of clarifying the wine share one drawback: They remove some of the heavier compounds that give flavor to the wine. Over-filtering or overfining can rob a wine of some of its complexity, so it is best done with a light hand. Some wineries bottle special batches of wine without any fining or filtering; these wines often form heavy sediments in the bottle, but the reward is a wine with more character.

Tasting, Blending, and Bottling

Making wine is not a simple matter of following a recipe, as brewing beer is. At regular intervals during the aging process, the winemaker tastes the wine to determine how long to age it; when to rack, fine, or filter; and when to bottle. A skilled winemaker can bring out the best qualities in each wine, largely by knowing what to do and when to do it (and when to leave it alone). Laboratory tests can give some clues about what is happening as the wine develops, but the final evaluation must be made by this one skilled individual.

One of the most important steps in this process is blending. Each growing year, each batch of wine, even each barrel has its own characteristics and presents its own challenges. Wines from different vineyards will show quite obvious differences. One may have plenty of fruit, but be a little low in acid; another, made from grapes picked a bit less ripe, might have too much acid. Together, they can make a balanced wine. Some wineries keep the best batches separate, bottling them as *special selection* or *reserve* wines; others may blend, letting the best wines raise the overall quality.

Bottling is the most mechanized step in the winemaking process. Modern machines can sterilize, fill, seal, label, and package thousands of bottles of wine per hour, allowing only a minimal exposure of the wine to air. After bottling, the wine needs some time to "rest," and most wineries store it for at least a month before shipping. Some wines are aged in the bottle for months or even years at wineries that can afford to tie up the space (and the capital). More often, wines are shipped as soon as they are stable, leaving the decision to age or not to age up to the customer.

Sparkling Wines

In the fermentation process, every molecule of sugar in the grape juice is split into one molecule of alcohol and one of carbon dioxide gas. In making table wines, all of this gas is allowed to escape before the wine is bottled. If the wine is bottled while a little sugar and yeast remain, however, the gas has nowhere to go and it stays in solution in the form of carbonic acid. When the bottle is opened, the gas forms the familiar bubbles that give the "sparkle" to Champagne and other sparkling wines, as well as to beer and carbonated soft drinks. (Although *Champagne* is widely used as a generic name for all sparkling wines, strictly speaking it refers only to a specific type of sparkling wine made in the Champagne region of France. See page 34 for a discussion of generic names for American wines.)

The first sparkling wines were most likely made by mistake. A batch of wine that was thought to be finished was bottled but continued to ferment inside the bottle. As the pressure built up, many of the bottles undoubtedly burst. But the bottles that survived held a wine that produced a delightful tingle on the tongue.

The modern process of making sparkling wines—the *méthode champenoise* or Champagne method—is traditionally credited to Dom Pérignon, a seventeenth-century French monk whose name is immortalized in a famous French Champagne, although others certainly shared in the discovery. By carefully checking the sugar level, using a heavier bottle, and tying down the cork with string or wire, Dom Pérignon and his colleagues made the first reliable sparkling wines.

SPARKLING WINE TERMS

While many American wineries make sparkling wines, few have been able to improve on the label terms used by the French. Here is a guide to the specialized language of Champagne and its imitators, starting with the degrees of sweetness:

Natural, au naturel   A label used by some wineries for totally dry sparkling wines, drier than brut.

Brut   The driest sparkling wines made by most houses. In theory they are completely dry, but some have as much as 1.5 percent residual sugar.

Extra dry   For some reason, people like to think that sparkling wines are less sweet than they really are. Extra dry wines are almost always noticeably sweet, with a residual sugar reading of 1.5 to 2.5 percent, but still less so than sec.

Sec   The French word translates as dry, but in practice sec sparkling wines are fairly sweet, with a residual sugar reading of 2 to 4 percent.

Dry   The English equivalent of sec; this term rarely appears on labels, but if it does, it should not be taken literally. The wine falls into the same category as sec above.

Demi-sec   Semidry; in practice, this means quite sweet (sweeter than sec). These wines register a residual sugar reading of 3.5 percent or more.

Other terms that may turn up in a discussion of sparkling wines are:

Blanc de blancs   Literally, "white from whites"; a white wine made from white grapes, such as Chardonnay.

Blanc de noirs   A white wine made from "black" grapes, such as Pinot Noir. Some have a slightly pink or coppery color.

Champagne   Strictly speaking, only the sparkling wines made in a legally defined area of the Champagne region of northern France. Unlike most of the world, the United States allows sparkling wines to carry names like *New York State Champagne* or *California Champagne*.

Cold Duck   A blend of white and red sparkling wines, usually fairly sweet and rarely very good.

Crémant   Literally "creaming"; a wine with less sparkle than normal sparkling wines. Crémant wines have less sugar added for the secondary fermentation, producing less gas pressure in the finished wine.

Cuvée   The blend of still wines that forms the base of any sparkling wine. The best sparkling wines begin with the best cuvées.

Dosage   The mixture of wine, sugar, and sometimes brandy added to the finished wine to give it the desired degree of body and sweetness.

Fermented in the bottle   Made by the transfer process.

Fermented in this bottle   Made by the *méthode champenoise*.

Méthode champenoise   The traditional, labor-intensive process that makes the finest sparkling wines.

Sparkling burgundy   A common American name for sparkling red wines, which, of course, have no more resemblance to true Burgundy than they do to Champagne.

In the laborious process known as riddling, sparkling-wine bottles are given a slight shake and a quarter turn every day, to help the yeast sediment settle into the necks. A paint mark on the bottom of each bottle helps keep track of which have been turned. An experienced cellar worker can riddle tens of thousands of bottles a day.

The best sparkling wines are now made by a slightly refined version of the process discovered by Dom Pérignon. In the modern Champagne method, the winemaker starts with a cuvée, or blend, of dry wines, then adds a carefully measured amount of sugar and yeast to the mixture and bottles it. The bottles are closed with a crown cap, then left on their sides to ferment again.

Once all the added sugar has disappeared through fermentation, the yeasts settle out of the wine. The problem now is to get the yeast sediment out of the wine but keep the bubbles in. This is done through a laborious process known as *riddling*. The bottles are set neck-down in special racks. Each day, each bottle is given a slight shake and a quarter turn and is tilted slightly closer to vertical. Eventually, all of the yeast sediment settles against the cap, and the wine is crystal clear, completely dry, and sparkling.

The next step, known as *disgorging*, removes the sediment from the bottles. The neck of each bottle is dipped in a freezing solution, which freezes a little bit of wine, trapping all of the sediment with it. The cap is then removed, and the pressure forces the plug of ice out. The bottle is quickly topped up with more of the same wine, then corked. The extra-large cork is wired down to keep it from popping out prematurely.

At the time it is disgorged, the wine is completely dry (that is, there is no sugar remaining). Many people prefer their sparkling wines somewhat sweet, so most wineries add some sugar to the wine at this point. The sugar, often with a touch of brandy mixed in, is dissolved in some of the same wine and this mixture (called the *dosage*) is used to top up the bottles after disgorging. Depending on how much sugar is added, the wine may be labeled *brut* (completely dry to a barely detectable sweetness); *extra dry* (usually with a noticeable sweetness); *sec* or *dry* (sweeter still); or *demi-sec* or *semidry* (very sweet). A few wineries whose brut wines are a little on the sweet side bottle some wine with absolutely no dosage, producing a bone-dry wine called *natural*.

The méthode champenoise is obviously quite labor-intensive, which helps account for the higher price of sparkling wines. (Higher taxes on sparkling wines add a share, too.) As a result, these wines proudly carry the words *méthode champenoise* or *fermented in this bottle* on their labels. However, there are less expensive methods that produce more affordable sparkling wines. One of these is known as the *transfer process*. It begins the same way as the méthode champenoise, with the secondary fermentation in individual bottles, but instead of undergoing riddling, the bottles are fed onto a special disgorging line. Here, in an automated process that resembles a reverse bottling line, the bottles are opened and the wine (always under pressure) is transferred to a large tank. After settling overnight, the wine is sterile-filtered, the dosage is added all at once to the whole batch, and the wine is put into the final bottles, corked, labeled, and packaged. (The extra-heavy bottles used for the secondary fermentation remain in the winery to be used over and over again.) Transfer-process wines may legally carry the label term *fermented in the bottle*, but only the Champagne-method labels may claim the wine is "fermented in *this* bottle."

The least expensive method, and the one that produces the vast majority of California sparkling wines, is the Charmat bulk process. Here, the cuvée of dry wines is assembled in a large tank, sugar and yeast are added, and the tank is sealed tight. As the sugar ferments, the gas is trapped, exactly as it is in the bottle. The finished sparkling wine is filtered, sweetened, and bottled just as in the transfer process.

Unfortunately, many people only drink sparkling wines at special occasions, like weddings, or use it for ritual purposes, like christening boats or celebrating sports victories. But sparkling wines are made to be enjoyed at the table, too. Even an inexpensive sparkling wine gives a festive touch to a meal, and it is hard to imagine a better apéritif than a glass of well-made brut. Keep a few bottles of sparkling wine in your wine cellar and you will always be ready for a celebration.

Special Note

CORKS AND OTHER CLOSURES

Until the eighteenth century, most wine was served from the barrel in pitchers or carafes. The development of a reliable seal, in the form of cork, made it possible to store and age individual bottles.

Cork is the spongy bark of an oak tree native to Spain and Portugal. Its elasticity allows it to squeeze into the neck of a bottle, then spring back to form a tight seal. As long as it is kept moist by contact with the wine, it will keep the wine in and air and spoilage organisms out for 20 years or more. Wines aged longer than this need to be recorked every few decades.

Like barrel aging, bottle aging is only partly understood, and one of the most controversial questions is the role of the cork. Some experts insist that a cork-finished bottle is more "alive" than a hermetically sealed one because the cork transmits small amounts of oxygen into the bottle. Others insist that air transfer through the cork is insignificant compared to the amount of air already in the bottle. Further research is unlikely to change many minds.

Occasionally, a flaw in the cork can allow wine to leak out and an unusual amount of air to get in, resulting in a spoiled wine. For this reason the cork is always presented for inspection before a bottle of wine is served in a restaurant (see page 55). The seal can also be ruined if the bottle is stored in an upright position for a long time, drying out the cork. By and large, though, corks have proven to be reliable.

There are, of course, other ways of sealing a wine bottle. Metal or plastic screw caps are cheap and reliable, but they are associated with inexpensive jug wines, making them undesirable for fine wines. Plastic stoppers for sparkling wines seem to be more acceptable to the consumer, although the more expensive sparkling wines still use a natural cork.

A wine cellar needn't contain dozens of cases. Once you begin tasting and enjoying wine, you may want to stock a small cellar with your favorite finds.

Stocking Your Cellar: Buying & Tasting Wine

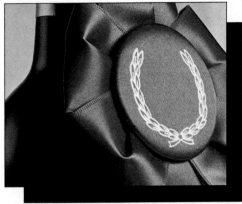

Purchasing wine—in a
restaurant, in a wine shop,
or at the winery itself—can
be confusing. In this chapter, you'll
find complete guidelines for selecting wines,
with helpful information on questions
such as vintage years, generic and
semigeneric names, bottle shapes, and price,
as well as advice on starting your
own wine cellar. The chapter also contains
a full discussion of wine tasting,
the pleasurable process of discovering
which wines you like. A
glossary of wine-tasting terms
appears on pages
44-45.

BUYING WINE

Your wine cellar can be as simple as a few bottles each of two or three favorite wines or it can include cases of wines put away for further aging. How much wine you buy for your cellar depends on many factors: storage space, how often you drink wine, and your budget, to name just a few. A cellar containing anywhere from a dozen bottles to dozens of cases, which you can replenish as you go along, can provide you with a steady supply of favorites. You don't actually have to have an underground cellar to start collecting wines—a cool closet will do (see "Storing Wine," pages 48-50).

WHERE TO BUY

Depending on where you live, wine may be available in specialty shops (liquor stores or wine shops), grocery stores, delicatessens, gift shops, or department stores. Wineries often sell directly to the public, either at the source or at shops in tourist areas. The choice of where to buy wines will depend on what you are looking for—price, selection, service, convenience, or a combination of all of these qualities.

Buying Wine at Retail

Supermarkets that carry wine have traditionally featured inexpensive, everyday wines, often in large jugs. In recent years, however, especially in major metropolitan wine markets, many supermarkets have begun to carry large selections of fine wines in addition to jug wines. Supermarkets often have competitive prices, but are essentially self-service; grocery clerks can rarely give you much information about unfamiliar wines. Still, supermarkets are a convenient place to buy the wines with which you are already familiar.

Specialty shops take the opposite approach, emphasizing service and knowledge of wines more than competitive pricing and convenience. In many cases, the owner or wine buyer has personally tasted most of the wines on the shelf and can describe them to the customer. Some states allow wine tasting in retail stores, either free or for a nominal cost.

For the customer who wants to know more about available wines, there is no better ally than a good wine merchant. Such a person is most likely to be found in a specialty wine shop or a well-stocked liquor store or department store.

Like a good butcher or fishmonger, a good wine merchant can be a valuable help. Someone who is willing to listen and make sound recommendations can help to find the perfect wine for your needs. There are several things to look for in a wine merchant:

Selection   The store should carry a selection of wines from various regions and producers and in various price ranges, rather than just one or two product lines.

Knowledgeable Service   Look for someone who is familiar with the wines and can describe them in terms that you can understand. Don't be afraid to ask if the salesperson has tasted a particular wine.

Handling and Storage   The wines should be stored and displayed so that they will not be damaged—mainly by heat or sunlight. Bottles of wine that do not sell rapidly should be stored on their sides or upside down in cases to prevent drying of the corks, which can lead to spoiled wine. White wines should be available from the shelf, not just from the refrigerator. (See pages 49-50 for more information on storage conditions.)

Tasting   If stores in your area are allowed to pour wines for tasting, this can provide an inexpensive way to sample several wines without buying a bottle of each.

Price   All other things being equal, it's nice to have a merchant who offers competitive prices.

Wine and Price   Prices of wines vary greatly, from a few dollars for a 3-liter jug to hundreds for rare bottles. What accounts for this spread?

The cost of producing a bottle of wine involves many factors. The price of grapes varies widely, with the most prestigious varieties costing three to four times the price of bulk blending varieties. Packaging costs (the bottle, cork, label, and carton) are more or less the same for any wine in a standard bottle with a cork, but screw-top jugs and bag-in-box packages are less expensive. Wines that require aging at the winery are necessarily more expensive than wines that can be shipped out a few months after the vintage; not only is there the cost of the barrels (which must be replaced after several years) to consider, but also the extra storage space and the money that is tied up in the wine while it sits in the cellar or warehouse. Wineries must spread these costs over the entire batch of wine, adding to the cost per bottle.

In fact, one of the biggest factors in the cost of wine is the cost of money. The current American "wine boom" involves massive amounts of capital investment, much of it borrowed at stiff interest rates. A vineyard takes almost a decade to produce a profit; the vines do not produce a decent crop until at least the third or fourth season, and it may take several more years to establish a reputation for quality that allows the grower to get the best price for the fruit. Wineries are also long-term investments; cash flows out for years before there is a product to sell. No wonder, then, that when a Chardonnay from a new winery appears on the market, it may be near the price of prestigious wines that have been known for years. Even at a high price, the winery is probably still losing money on the wine.

Labor costs take their share of the price of each bottle. There are economies of scale in the larger wineries; on the other hand, small wineries are often a "labor of love" in which the proprietor's time and effort are drastically underpaid. Distribution costs and taxes are relatively independent of the price of the wine, being based on volume.

The final element in the price of wine is the hardest to calculate—prestige. Certain wines have a reputation for quality, in most cases well deserved, that increases the price the public is willing to pay. Production costs certainly vary, but what ultimately allows one winery to charge $20 for its Cabernet and its neighbor only $7 is simple supply and demand. If enough people are willing to pay the price of the more expensive wine, the price will never come down.

How much, then, should a good bottle of wine cost? The answer depends entirely on the buyer. In any given price range, there are bound to be some wines that you like better than others. There are very likely some that you would prefer to many more expensive ones. The smartest buyers will concentrate on wines within the price range in which they are comfortable, with an eye out for bargains at any price. Some inexperienced buyers make the mistake of assuming that they have to pay a lot of money to find a wine that they will like. Spending twice what you would ordinarily spend on a bottle of wine for a special occasion can lead to disappointment, if it does not measure up to your increased expectations. It would be far better to choose a familiar wine that you can serve with pride.

The same rule applies on occasions when you need to serve inexpensive wines, say for an open house or some other large event. Even if you do not drink "jug" wines regularly, it is a good idea to have a few favorites that you can serve with confidence. A good merchant should be able to recommend wines in any price range. By all means taste the wine ahead of time; it is certainly worth the investment in one jug to make sure that the wine is one you would want to drink before you serve it to fifty guests.

A well-stocked wine shop contains a wide selection of wines. A knowledgeable salesperson can be of great help in finding just the right bottle.

Better restaurants generally offer a selection of wines chosen to complement their menus. Your waiter can be your guide in choosing an appropriate wine to enhance your meal. In the fanciest restaurants, this is the job of the wine steward, or sommelier, who may wear the traditional "badge" of the wine steward, a silver tasting cup on a chain.

Buying Wine at the Source

A day in the "wine country" can be a pleasant way to learn a little about wine and how it is made, and it offers the chance to taste before you buy. Most of the medium- to large-sized wineries offer public tours that can give the novice a good feel for how wine is made. The harvest season is the most enjoyable and informative time for a winery tour, but winemakers often have little time for visitors then. Tours typically end in the tasting room, where complimentary samples of some or all of the wines are poured. Where state and local laws allow, the wines are available for sale in the tasting room, which may double as a gift shop.

Don't expect to save a lot of money by buying wines at the source.

For various reasons—overhead and labor costs of tasting rooms and winery tours, the cost of all the wine poured as free samples, and a desire not to undersell their retailers—most wineries sell their wines at the normal retail price. Sometimes they have special lots of wine that are only offered for sale at the winery, but in general they offer the same selection at the same prices as you'll find in retail shops.

Depending on the winery, the visitor may be offered tastes of two or three chosen varieties or may select from the winery's entire line. Tasting a lot of different wines in one session can be confusing to the palate (not to mention the memory!), so you might want to limit your tasting to a few varieties, and compare them to other wineries' versions of the same types. The result will be more informative than tasting wines at random.

For the novice, the wineries offering a wide range of wines are the best places to start. If you have some idea of what kinds of wines you like—red or white; sweet, dry, or in-between; light or full-bodied—the tasting room hosts can steer you in the right direction. One large winery, Almaden in San Jose, California, has come up with a novel approach: The first step in their tasting room is a "blind" tasting (one in which the identities of the wines are not disclosed) of three wines ranging from dry to fairly sweet. Based on their preferences among these three wines, customers are directed toward one group or another of Almaden's large line of wines, and away from those they are less likely to enjoy.

In some areas, notably California's Napa Valley, so many wine lovers visit the popular wineries that they create traffic jams on weekends. Occasionally, there is talk of trying to reduce the number of tourists, but the tasting rooms are an essential part of public relations for most major wineries. They also account for a lot of wine sales.

Buying Wine in Restaurants

Choosing the most appropriate wine can sometimes be an imposing task for the restaurant customer. Wine lists run the gamut from a single hand-written page to huge leather-bound volumes, and the wines may or may not be well matched to the menu. How is the customer to choose?

There are many ways to approach a restaurant wine list, but they all come down to three choices in the end: You can select familiar wines, take your chances on something new, or ask for help. The first approach is the safest, the second the most risky. The third may be the best, assuming the waiters are knowledgeable.

In the best restaurants, the wines on the list are carefully chosen to complement the menu, and wines that need bottle aging may be held for several years before even appearing on the list. On the other hand, many restaurateurs, especially those not familiar with wines, opt for a *wholesaler's list*—a standard assortment of one brand, or at most two or three brands, distributed by the same company that supplies most of the liquor. Between these extremes are the wine lists that combine the restaurateur's personal choices with popular, widely known wines.

Whether the wine list contains a dozen wines or a hundred, chances are that there will be unfamiliar wines on it. Like a good wine merchant, a good waiter should be able to tell you something about each of the wines. Better restaurants train their waiters to be familiar with the wines and to make recommendations for specific wines with specific dishes on the menu. In larger, more formal restaurants, there is an employee (the wine steward or *sommelier*) who is in charge of the wine list and wine service. Don't be afraid to ask for recommendations, but don't let yourself be talked into a wine you don't really want either.

Finding mature wines, especially red wines, on restaurant wine lists can be difficult. Few small restaurants have the space to age a large quantity of wine, nor can most of them afford to tie up a lot of money in cellared wine. Many restaurants have an impressive list of young Cabernets, for example, but most are years away from their optimum drinking age. This is less of a problem with white wines, though some Chardonnays can age well beyond the time that they have disappeared from retail shelves and wine lists.

Once you have made your selection, the waiter will pour a small amount of the wine for approval by the person who ordered the wine (see "The Ritual of the Cork," page 55). There are two circumstances in which a bottle can and should be rejected: if it is clearly spoiled (vinegary or moldy in smell or taste) or if it is not the way it was described (noticeably sweet, for example, if the waiter or wine list described it as dry). If you encounter either of these situations, just inform the waiter that the wine is unacceptable. In the first case, another bottle of the same type should be brought; in the second, make another choice. Occasionally, an awkward situation arises when a wine is sound, but not to the customer's taste. Restaurants really can't be expected to take these wines back; just chalk it up to experience and choose more carefully the next time.

Naturally, restaurateurs want you to enjoy your meal, and wine adds to the enjoyment. But more than that, wine generates a great deal of profit for the restaurant. The markup varies from one restaurant to the next, but double the retail price (roughly three times the wholesale cost) and more is not unusual for bottled wines. The markup on "house wine" by the glass or carafe can be much higher. This is not meant to imply that restaurant

owners are greedy; food and labor are very expensive, and without the revenue from wine and liquor, many restaurants would not be profitable at all. Still, it is disturbing to see a wine on the list for $15 when you can buy it at a retail price of $6 to $7.

Some restaurants, especially newer ones in major wine markets, sell their wines at a lower markup. A few have gone a step farther, charging the standard retail markup and adding a few dollars to cover the service costs. So far, the customer reaction has been positive, and restaurants that have changed to this price structure usually report greater wine sales.

Another welcome trend is to offer better wines by the glass as well as by the full bottle. If you are the only one in your group that wants a white wine, or if you are dining alone, it is nice to be able to order a good glass of wine, rather than the house wine (which tends to be the least expensive brand of generic red, white, or rosé the owner finds drinkable). Many customers would gladly pay twice as much for a glass of a good-quality Chardonnay or Chenin Blanc than a nondescript Chablis.

There may be times when you want to bring your own wine to a restaurant. It may be an older bottle from your cellar, a special wine that has sentimental value, or a wine that the restaurant does not stock. Most restaurants will allow this, but it is customary (and quite reasonable) to add a "corkage" fee to your bill. The corkage fee varies according to the price range of the restaurant, but it is typically a small amount. However, some restaurants charge high corkage fees to discourage customers from bringing their own wine—after all, they would rather sell a bottle from their list—and they may resist serving a customer's wine if it is on their list. Thus, if you want to bring your own wine, it is wisest to call ahead and to determine the corkage fee and policy in advance.

HOW TO GET THE WINE YOU WANT

Once you find a store with a good selection and helpful staff, you still have some work to do in order to take advantage of the salesclerks' knowledge. The better you know what you want and how to ask for it, the easier it will be for the merchant to find it. The first step is to identify your own tastes and the kinds of wine you like. It will also help to learn the basic terms used in wine tasting, such as sweet versus dry, and high acid versus low acid. (See "Tasting Wine," beginning on page 37, and especially the glossary of wine-tasting terms on pages 44-45.)

One good way to establish a rapport with a wine merchant is to show him a dinner menu you plan to serve, complete with sauces and seasonings, and ask for a wine recommendation to go with it. If the combination works, by all means tell him so! Take along another menu and ask for another recommendation. Before long the merchant may be setting aside a good bottle or two for you.

Every once in a while, you may get a bottle you don't like. In certain cases, the wine may actually be spoiled. A wine that smells strongly like vinegar or has a moldy smell or taste is spoiled, either through poor winemaking or poor storage. In either case, you should be able to return the opened bottle to the place you bought it for a refund. (The merchant will then return it to the supplier for credit.)

But what about a bottle that is not spoiled, but that you find unpleasant? Again, it can't hurt to take it back to the store. The merchant may not offer a refund (in some states this is illegal except for clearly damaged wine), but he or she may help you identify what it is you don't like (say, high natural acid) and steer you away from similar wines in the future. Before you pour a "bad" bottle of wine down the sink, see if there is something you can learn from it.

HOW MUCH TO BUY?

Many people buy wine the same way they buy bread or milk or canned beans—whenever they need some. However, there are advantages to buying wine less often and in a greater quantity.

The biggest advantage is convenience. Once you have decided that you like a wine, it is much easier to pull a bottle out of your own stock than it is to run to the store for one. Even with a jug wine that is perpetually in stock at your grocer's, it's nice to have a backup bottle on hand.

If your favorite wines are not always available, you may want to stock up on them when you can. Large wineries generally make enough of each of their wines to last until the next vintage or blend is ready to release, but smaller wineries often run out between releases. Nothing is more frustrating than discovering a new favorite, only to find that the last case sold out a week ago.

Frequently money can be saved by buying wine in quantity. Most retailers give a discount (typically 10 percent) on a case of 12 bottles of the same wine; some will give the same discount on a mixed case of several wines. When wines go "on sale" at special prices (in markets where prices are not controlled), buying a case or more of a favorite wine can save you quite a bit of money.

The decision of how much of a particular wine to buy will depend on the storage space available and your own preference. Do you like to drink the same one or two wines day in and day out, or do you prefer more variety? Do you intend to drink the wine soon, or put some of it away for longer aging? If the wine is of limited availability, how much are you likely to drink before the next time it is available? Answering these questions for yourself before you buy can help you develop a cellar of manageable size, full of your favorite wines.

HOW TO READ A WINE LABEL

Wine labels are as individual and distinctive as the wines inside the bottles. Federal and state regulations require that certain information appear on the label of every bottle of wine. Most winemakers go beyond the requirements, however, because the label is one of the most important parts of the winery's image. Knowing how to read a label can provide a lot of useful information about the wine.

By federal law, every bottle of wine must bear the following information:

Bottler gives the name and location of the bottler of the wine. By itself, *bottled by* does not mean that the bottling winery crushed and fermented any of the wine; they may simply have bought the wine in bulk from another producer and bottled it. *Made and bottled by* means the bottling winery crushed and fermented at least 10 percent of the wine; *produced and bottled by* means that at least 75 percent of the wine was crushed and fermented at the bottling winery. If the winery produced 100 percent of the wine, and the grapes came entirely from vineyards owned or controlled by the winery, then the winery is entitled to use the designation *grown, produced, and bottled by.* Most wineries prefer to be directly involved in the total process, from the vineyard to the bottle, although there are excellent wines sold by wineries that buy, age, and blend wines crushed by other wineries.

Type of Wine indicates the general or specific category of wine in the bottle. This may be a generic name, such as *red table wine;* a proprietary name coined by the winery, such as Vichon's "Chevrignon," a combination of Chevrier (Semillon) and Sauvignon Blanc; a semigeneric name, such as *burgundy* or *chablis;* or a varietal name, that is, the name of the predominant grape variety. Varietal wines, to be labeled such, must

contain at least 75 percent of the named variety; and many are, in fact, 100 percent varietal. Blends of more than one variety may carry the varietal names and percentage of each on the label. Generic wines are typically made of a blend of varieties, which may or may not be listed on the label. Proprietary names are typically followed by a varietal or generic name, whichever is appropriate.

Alcohol Content gives the amount of alcohol in the wine, expressed as a percentage of volume. The exact content may vary 1½ percent from the figure on the label; thus, a wine labeled 12½ percent alcohol may actually have anywhere from 11 to 14 percent alcohol. A few wineries use the designation "table wine," which covers a range from 7 to 14 percent. Fortified wines typically contain from 18 to 20 percent alcohol.

Net Contents The standard bottle size is now 750 milliliters (25.4 fluid ounces), the same as in most of Europe. (The former standard was the fifth, ⅕ of a gallon, or 25.6 ounces.) Half-gallon and gallon jugs have been replaced by 1.5-liter and 3- or 4-liter sizes. The net contents need not be on the label if it is embossed on the bottle, as it usually is.

Beyond the required information, a number of other items are typically found on labels. Some of these are useful to the consumer, while others are merely decorative or promotional. The important features are:

Vintage Year This date indicates that all the grapes were harvested during the stated year. The word *vintage* may or may not appear; it has no additional meaning.

Some labels are simple, others more elaborate. Certain elements are required by law: (1) the name of the winery that bottled the wine; (2) the type of wine, which may be a grape name, a proprietary name, or a generic term; (3) the alcohol content; and (4) the net contents (either on the label or on the bottle itself). Also typically included are (5) the geographic source of the grapes and (6) a vintage year, if applicable. If the wine comes from a particular vineyard, that may also be noted on the label (7). The specific varietal blend (8) may be listed, but is not required. A few labels include the winemaker's notes—items such as how the wine was made, how long to let it age, which foods to serve with it, and so on (9).

GENERICS AND SEMIGENERICS

Chablis, Burgundy, Rhine, Sauternes, Champagne, Chianti, port, sherry—all of these are names of European wines of world-famous quality, recognized as the products of specific areas and specific grapes. Each of these names is legally protected in almost every country except the United States, Australia, and South Africa. All of these names have been appropriated at one time or another for American wines. The semigeneric names typical of large California and New York wineries are an unfortunate vestige of the early days of the American wine industry, when winemakers thought nothing of borrowing the names of the most famous winemaking regions of Europe for wines that were only vaguely similar to their European cousins. Some have dropped out of wide usage, but several remain, to the chagrin of winemakers in Europe whose fortunes rest on the reputation of the real things.

Fortunately, the finest American wines are now known by varietal names such as Cabernet Sauvignon (see list on pages 106–112). In addition, many conscientious producers of generic wines have dropped the semigeneric European names in favor of true generic names, like red table wine or white table wine.

Source of Grapes Although it is not required, most wines carry an appellation of the origin, or geographic source, of the grapes. This may be a state, a county, or a viticultural area. The last category is a recent invention, and refers to "a significant grape-growing region whose geography and boundaries are recognized and strictly defined by the federal government." By law, wines with a state or county appellation must be at least 75 percent from vineyards within the state or county. For a viticultural-area label, the requirement is 85 percent.

Viticultural-area labeling was established in 1978 as a means of regulating the trend of identifying wines with the specific areas in which their grapes were grown. It is modeled, to a certain extent, on European "controlled appellation" laws. The European wine-growing nations have strict legal controls on the use of place-names on wine labels, to protect the quality reputation of certain sites known to produce fine wines. *Appellation contrôlée* on a French label or *denominazione di origine controllata* on an Italian label is a guarantee that the wine came from a given location, and it usually implies that certain grape varieties were used and traditional vineyard and winemaking procedures were followed.

The American laws are much less restrictive, but they stem from the same desire to identify and recognize the specific locations where certain grape varieties produce the best wines. The Carneros region of southern Napa and Sonoma counties is an example. For a long time it was thought to be too cool to ripen grapes, being close to the ocean air and chilling fogs coming through the Golden Gate and San Francisco Bay. But experimental plantings of Pinot Noir and Chardonnay, two early-ripening varieties well suited to cooler areas, produced excellent wines.

Wineries began to add "Carneros" or "Carneros District" to their Napa Valley or Sonoma Valley wines made from this area, and the wines were well received in the market. Los Carneros is now an officially recognized viticultural area straddling the Napa-Sonoma county line, and it produces some of the finest Pinot Noirs and Chardonnays in California. Most of these wines also carry the Napa Valley or Sonoma Valley appellation, referring to the larger viticultural areas within which the Carneros region falls.

Like vintage dates, specific viticultural-area labels do not themselves ensure quality. Excellent Rieslings, for example, are made with the simple appellation *Washington* rather than the more restrictive *Yakima Valley* label. A wine labeled *Dry Creek Valley* (a region of Sonoma County) is not necessarily better than another simply labeled *Sonoma County*. In the long run, the skill of the grower and winemaker is as important as the source of the grapes. But there is no doubt that viticultural-area appellations are letting the consumer play a bigger role in the process of matching the best grape to the best location.

Special Designations Wineries may label particular batches of wine with the name of the specific vineyard, or a term like *private reserve* or *special selection*. These terms have no legal definition; they generally represent the best or most distinctive wines the winery has to offer. They almost always carry a higher price, and it is up to the consumer to decide if the difference in quality is worth the extra price. Bear in mind also that red "reserve" wines are often the biggest, most tannic, longest-lived wines the winery makes. Many of them will need several more years of bottle age to reach their best drinkability.

Estate bottled is one term that does have a legal definition: It means, first, that the winery crushed, fermented, and bottled 100 percent of the wine on its own premises; and second, that the wine is entirely from vineyards owned or controlled by the winery and located within the same viticultural area as the winery. (In the past, a few wineries made "estate bottled" wines from their vineyards hundreds of miles away, which suggests a rather large "estate.")

Technical Information Some wine labels include a lot of information about the wine, not all of which is of interest to the consumer. Of the detailed chemical analyses sometimes given, only the residual-sugar level is really important to most of us. Residual-sugar readings on the label are especially useful on white wines such as Riesling, Gewürztraminer, and Chenin Blanc, which range widely from completely dry (no residual sugar) to fairly sweet (anywhere from 1 to 3 percent residual sugar, and even more for "late-harvest" types).

Information such as the harvest date of the grapes, the sugar and acid levels at harvest, the type of cooperage used to age the wine, and the number of bottles or cases produced may be of interest to the winery, but it rarely influences the decision to buy a bottle or the buyer's enjoyment of the wine.

Aesthetics One of the most important roles of the label, from the winery's point of view, is to create an image. Some prefer a style of understated elegance, others choose exuberant designs. Many labels feature pictures of the winery building or the landscape around it. Some give an abundance of "consumer information" or expound their owner's philosophy on wine, while others keep it simple and let the wines speak for themselves. No one approach is correct; each label is as individual as the wine inside the bottle.

VINTAGE YEARS AND "VINTAGE WINES"

One of the most misunderstood words in the wine business is *vintage*. In its strictest definition, it is a noun that describes the process of harvesting, crushing, and fermenting the year's grape crop. If all of the grapes used to make a given wine are harvested in the same year, the wine may carry a vintage date. The presence or absence of a vintage date does not have anything to do with quality, yet the word *vintage* has come to have a connotation of quality: We hear of "vintage" automobiles and "vintage jazz." The image is one of outstanding, enduring quality. No wonder most wineries like to have vintage dates on their labels.

The reason wines carry vintage dates is that each year's growing conditions are unique. Sunshine, heat, and rainfall vary; the relative amounts and timing can make the difference between perfectly ripe fruit and underripe, overripe, or moldy grapes. Vintage dates are especially important in colder areas, where grapes do not ripen fully every year and perfect conditions may only occur two or three times in each decade. The variation between vintages in Germany or Burgundy, for example, directly affects prices, with great vintages commanding much higher prices than those from poor years.

Certain wines of Europe, notably Champagne and port, are only given vintage dates in the best years, and the wines of lesser years are blended. *Vintage years* in these districts are those which produce wines good enough to be bottled without blending, which may be responsible for the general (but mistaken) idea that vintage-dated wines are always better than nonvintage wines.

Not long ago, the California wine industry made the misleading boast that "every year is a vintage year in California." This was an oversimplification, but in one sense it was true: In the mild climate of California, ripeness is rarely a problem, and growers can be confident of bringing in a crop almost every year.

Still, there are differences between vintages even in areas with mild climates. For instance, in too warm a growing season, the grapes will ripen quickly but with little flavor; too much rain at harvest time may cause the grapes to swell with water, diluting the flavor, or worse still, to become moldy. Perfect conditions, in which the grapes ripen with just the right balance of flavor, sugar, and acid, simply do not occur every year in every vineyard, any more than they do in Europe's finest vineyards.

Until recently, many of the better American wines were blends of several vintages. Blending has several advantages. If one year produces high-acid, lighter wine, and the following year's is rich and ripe but lacking in acid, blending the two carefully can produce a wine that is better balanced than either one alone. Blending a bit of older wine with a young wine of the same type gives smoothness and complexity to the wine. With skillful blending, a winery can achieve a consistent style from one year to the next, an essential feature of the most successful generic brands.

Yet within the last decade or so, nonvintage wines have all but disappeared from the premium wine market. Even wineries that were famous for the consistent quality of their blended varietal wines, such as Christian Brothers, have converted to vintage-dated wines in response to consumer demand. Whether consumers actually appreciate the subtle distinctions between vintages or simply associate vintage dates with higher quality is an open question. At any rate, nonvintage wines (other than generics and jug wines) now seem to be out of fashion.

Commonly used bottle shapes: Burgundy (1); Bordeaux, 750ml (2) and 1.5-liter "magnum" (3); all-purpose 375ml "tenth" (4); German or "Rhine" style (5); Champagne (6); port and sherry (7).

Bottle Shapes

Bottle shapes traditional for various European wines tend to be used here for similar styles of wine. Thus, in addition to the label, the bottle itself can suggest what is inside.

Tall, slender green or brown bottles are used in Alsace, most of Germany, and much of northern Italy. American wines made from the grapes typical of these regions (Riesling, Gewürztraminer, various Muscats) are generally sold in a similar bottle. Other fruity, flowery whites, particularly Chenin Blancs, may also be found in tall bottles; in clear glass, it is popular for rosés.

A shorter, stouter bottle with sloping shoulders is the standard for the wines of Burgundy and of the Loire and Rhône valleys. Wines made here from the Burgundian grapes (Pinot Noir, Chardonnay, Pinot Blanc, Gamay, Gamay Beaujolais) are almost always put into this type of bottle, as are wines from Syrah and Petite Sirah grapes (native to the Rhône), various French-American hybrid wines, and many generic reds and whites. A clear version is often used for rosés and blanc de noirs.

The straight-sided, square-shouldered bottle used in France's Bordeaux region and most of Italy is almost *de rigueur* for American wines made from Bordeaux grapes (Cabernet Sauvignon, Merlot, and, in the clear bottle, Sauvignon Blanc and Semillon). It is also typical for Zinfandel, Barbera, and generic wines made in a "claret" or "Italian" style. Some California ports meant for long bottle aging are put in this one, which stacks well in bins. Otherwise, dessert wines such as port and sherry, like their European models, usually have a bottle that looks like a stouter version of the Bordeaux one.

The heavy bottle of Champagne, designed to withstand pressure, is standard for American sparkling wines. Some wineries have adopted a clear bottle for these wines, especially those with a blush of color.

TASTING WINE

Tasting wine can be as simple or as complicated as you want, but it is always based on a simple distinction: "I like it" or "I don't like it."

There are many ways to "taste" wines. Whether examining a wine critically or simply quaffing it as a beverage, we taste the wine in a passive way with every sip, just as we taste foods; that is, we perceive varying sensations on the tongue and in the nose. But there is another, more active form of tasting that we do when trying an unfamiliar wine, or deciding whether to buy a few bottles, or when a bottle of wine is poured in a restaurant. This sensory evaluation of the wine is the kind of tasting this chapter discusses.

WINE AND THE SENSES

Wine tasting involves four senses—sight, smell, taste, and touch. We base our subjective judgments of quality on the information our senses provide; our brains perceive abstract qualities such as complexity, harmony, and balance in the way sensory impressions interact.

The first impression of the wine in the glass is visual. The color and clarity of the wine give the first clues to its soundness or to potential faults in the flavor.

Most of our sensory impressions of wine come from our sense of smell. Sniffing the wine before tasting provides one set of stimuli to the olfactory nerves located in the upper nose. Other odors reach the nose after sipping and even after swallowing the wine, through a narrow passage rising from the back of the mouth. Minute variations in hundreds of organic compounds give each wine its particular "aroma" and "bouquet" (see "Glossary of Tasting Terms," pages 44-45).

The taste receptors on the tongue (the "taste buds") are only capable of distinguishing four tastes: sweet, sour (acid), bitter, and salty. Generally, only the first three are involved in the taste of wine. Most of the other elements of the flavor of the wine are actually odors perceived in the nose.

The tongue, gums, and palate also receive tactile (touch) impressions that contribute to the flavor. These include "body"—the apparent "weight" of the wine—and astringency, the puckery, mouth-drying sensation produced by tannins in young wines.

THE TASTING RITUAL— SENSE AND NONSENSE

Wine tasting and wine tasters are easy targets for parody. Writers and cartoonists love to make fun of "wine experts" with furrowed brows peering into glasses, intently sniffing, sipping, and savoring the wine, and finally making mysterious pronouncements like "plenty of varietal character" and "complex nose."

However, there are reasons for all that swirling and sniffing. The tasting process is a series of steps, each of which focuses the senses on a particular aspect of the wine. Let's take a look at each of the steps and see how they contribute to the overall impression of the wine.

Appearance Pour a small serving (1 to 2 ounces) of wine into a clear, stemmed wine glass with a capacity of at least 6 ounces. When you are tasting more than one wine, the amounts in the glasses should be equal. Tilt the glass away from you, preferably over a white surface. Notice the tint, the depth of color, and the clarity of the wine.

One aspect of evaluating a wine is observing its color and clarity. Whether it is a straw-colored white, a coppery blanc de noirs, a purplish young red, or a brick-red aged wine, it should be brilliantly clear, with an attractive, pure color.

<u>*White Wine*</u> Is the color in the yellow range, or does it tend toward the green side (sometimes true of very young wines) or the amber side (a sign of more age or extreme concentration, as in sweet late-harvest wines)? Is there any hint of brown in the color (a bad sign, indicating that the wine may be too old or oxidized)? Is the wine brilliantly clear, or is it hazy or cloudy (a sign of suspended protein, which is generally a fault)?

<u>*Red Wine*</u> Is the color ruby red, or does it show purple tones (to be expected in young reds) or an amber-brown edge (appropriate for older wines)? Look at the depth of the color. Does it get darker toward the center, or is it pale (perhaps a sign of a watery-tasting wine)? Is the wine brilliant or hazy? (In an older wine, cloudy appearance may be the result

of sediment settling out of the wine, which can be eliminated by careful decanting—see page 57.)

<u>*Rosé, Vin Gris, or Blanc de Noirs*</u>
Is the color some shade of pink, salmon, or copper, without any trace of brown? Is the wine brilliant?

One truly silly tradition of wine tasting is looking at how the wine runs down the side of the glass after swirling. Some wines wash down quickly, while others cling to the glass, forming into thick or thin streams called "legs." True, thicker "legs" indicate a higher level of alcohol, but in themselves, do not necessarily add to the enjoyment of the wine. "Great legs" are not going to save a wine that doesn't taste good, or make a good wine taste better.

Aroma and Bouquet Swirl the glass two or three times to wash the wine up onto the sides of the glass. This increases the surface area of the wine, allowing its odors to escape into the air in the glass. Quickly bring the glass to your nose and inhale. Does the wine smell like grapes and like wine? Are there aromas suggesting other fruits, or flowers, herbs, spices? Are there any unpleasant odors or prickly sensations in your nose? Most important, does the smell of the wine invite you to take a sip?

Flavor Sip the wine and hold it in your mouth, rolling it around onto all parts of your tongue before swallowing. Is it sweet or dry, or right on the edge between the two? Is there enough acidity to leave the palate feeling clean and to balance any sweetness, or does the wine leave a coating or cloying sensation? Does the wine feel light or heavy on your tongue (indicating low or high body)? Is the wine astringent, like strong tea or an unripe persimmon (normal in young wines, but a sign that the wine needs more aging)? If there is any bitterness, is it in harmony with the other flavors, or is it unpleasant? Are all the elements in balance, or do some qualities dominate? After swallowing, does the flavor persist, or does it disappear quickly? All in all, is it a pleasant-tasting wine?

Of all the aspects of the tasting ritual, the easiest to make fun of are the various descriptions of the wines. Some tasters get very technical: "good sugar-acid balance, medium body, slight touch of sulfur dioxide."

Others go for free association: "splendid, ripe peach-honey aromas with overtones of vanilla . . ." Others rely on anthropomorphic traits: "young and exuberant, but unmistakably well-bred . . ." In each case, these terms may mean a great deal to the person who uses them, but they may be lost on others. If your goal is to communicate your impressions to others, try to stick to commonly understood terms, such as those in the glossary on pages 44–45.

The complex aromas of wines are often reminiscent of other foods. Cabernet Sauvignon (left above) may be compared to green olives, eucalyptus, black currant, mint, and bell pepper; mature wines may suggest violets, chocolate, coffee, tea, or truffles. Zinfandel is almost always described as berrylike, and Pinot Noir has an aroma of sweet spices and cherries, plums, or prunes. Chardonnay (right above) reminds tasters of apples, peaches, or pears, or of citrus, citrus blossoms, or honey. Barrel-aged Chardonnays are often likened to toast, butter, or vanilla.

One such numerical method for wine scorecards is the "Davis scale," developed at the University of California at Davis. The 20-point Davis scale awards and subtracts points for specific virtues and flaws, with a score of 20 denoting a perfect wine. Other scales used by professional tasters may have a perfect score of anywhere from 9 to 100 points.

The following is an example of a modified Davis scale, as used by a wine tasting organization in San Francisco:

Appearance	*0-2*
Color	*0-2*
Aroma and bouquet	*0-4*
Acescence	*0-2*
Total acid	*0-2*
Sugar	*0-1*
Body	*0-1*
Flavor	*0-2*
Astringency	*0-2*
General quality	*0-2*

A final score of 17–20: outstanding quality. 13–16: good commercial wine. 10–12: commercially acceptable with a notable defect. 0–9: commercially unacceptable.

This scale awards points for positive qualities and withholds them for negative traits. For example, a dull or hazy wine receives no points for appearance, while a brilliantly clear wine rates 2 points. "Acescence" is a technical term for an acetic acid (vinegar) aroma, sometimes listed on tasting forms as "volatile acidity." Wine with a strong vinegar aroma would receive a 0 for acescence, wine which has a trace of volatile acidity but is still enjoyable rates 1 point, and wine with no trace of the offending odor gets the full 2 points. Sugar, body, and astringency are all judged according to the wine type; residual sugar is out of place in a red wine, just as tannic astringency would be a fault in a light, slightly sweet white wine. General quality allows for the taster's overall subjective opinion of the wine. Some tasters modify their scorecards to give more weight to subjective quality.

Tasting wine can take many forms. In addition to comparing several wines of the same type, try an assortment of wines with a favorite menu and see how each wine combines with each food.

SCORECARDS AND TASTING NOTES

Unless you have an exceptional memory, you probably will not remember your impressions of wines for long. Taking notes on your tasting experiences is the best way to preserve this information.

Most professional wine tasters use a standard form for their written tasting notes to assure that all wines tasted will be judged on the same basis. This sort of standardization is especially important in a comparative tasting, where a group of wines are to be ranked. To arrive at a ranking, wine judges generally use a scorecard that assigns numerical values to the various tasting criteria—color, clarity, aroma, bouquet, and so on.

An easier way to use a 20-point scale is to start with a base score of 12, then add or subtract points according to specific qualities or faults:

Appearance
(color and clarity)   *0-4*
Scoring: 3 points for ordinary sound wine; add 1 for exceptional clarity or brilliance; subtract 1 or more for deficiencies in color or clarity.

Aroma and Bouquet   *0-6*
Scoring: 4 points for ordinary sound wine; add points for varietal aroma, bouquet; subtract points for off odors or acescence.

Flavor   *0-8*
Scoring: 5 points for ordinary sound wine; add points for varietal flavor, balance, depth; subtract points for off flavors or imbalance.

General Quality   *0-2*
Scoring: No additional points for average or below-average wine; 1 point for recommendable wine; 2 points for outstanding wine.

A tasting scale as detailed as the Davis scale is not very useful or meaningful to the average wine drinker. However, you may still want to distinguish among various levels of quality in the wines you taste. As mentioned earlier, the most important distinction is simple: You either like the wine or you don't. A useful scale for the average wine taster might have five levels: outstanding, above average, ordinary, below average, and unacceptable.

Whatever scale you use to rate wines, the purpose of tasting notes is the same: to help keep track of your tasting impressions for future reference. Using the same form for each tasting is helpful. Some wine lovers use forms that fit into loose-leaf binders or card files, and there are probably some enophiles with home computers who keep their tasting notes in electronic form.

Special Note

GOING FOR THE GOLD: WINE COMPETITIONS

In recent years, there has been an explosion of heavily publicized wine judgings at county fairs, harvest festivals, and other gatherings. Each fair awards its own set of medals, generally the familiar gold, silver, and bronze variety, but some go beyond to "double gold" or "platinum" medals. Wineries that win awards for their wines are quick to let the public know about it, with special stickers on the bottles or shelf tags proclaiming their triumphs.

Does the fact that a wine won a gold medal mean it is a superior wine? Sometimes. But there are several complicating factors. Some fairs are notoriously generous with their medals, while others are relatively stingy. A gold medal wine from one fair might not even get an honorable mention at another. With the dozens of competitions held each year, it seems that just about every winery can boast of a medal for at least one of its wines.

Another problem is the tendency to give high ranks to the most assertive wines while passing over more reserved, perhaps even better balanced, wines. In part, this results from the sheer volume of entries. In a major contest, it would not be unusual for over a hundred Chardonnays, for instance, to be competing with one another. Even with qualified professional judges, some very good wines are likely to be overlooked. It is no secret that "big" wines dominated tastings in the late 1970s and early 1980s. However, the tide seems to be turning now as judges appear to have begun to look for finesse rather than for power.

A medal in a major competition does not necessarily mean that the wine is the best in its category. Many wineries, including some of the best, refuse to enter their wines in any competition at all, and others are quite selective about which ones they enter. In fact, the fairs sometimes seem to be dominated by new labels, with wines from some of the older, more established wineries conspicuously absent.

The most important thing to remember about the results of any competitive tasting is that they represent the opinion of one particular set of judges on one particular day. The winning of a single medal does not guarantee a great wine. However, a consensus of several tastings is a good sign. If a wine consistently wins awards, it means that a large number of judges agree that it represents one of the best of its type. On the other hand, the results of even twenty tastings are only valid for you if they agree with your tastes. A certain vineyard's Cabernet may have taken a couple of gold medals here, a double gold there, and a Sweepstakes Award over there, but if you don't like Cabernet, you probably won't enjoy it. Even if you do like Cabernets in general, you might not like that particular wine. As always, let your taste be the ultimate judge.

LEARNING TO TASTE WINE: SOME STRATEGIES FOR BEGINNERS

Learning to taste wine is as much a process of learning about your own tastes as it is a process of learning to recognize aromas and flavors. However subtle or intellectual the tasting process becomes, the goal is always to decide whether or not you like a particular wine. Experts with years of tasting experience may describe a wine differently than you do, but who cares? Remember, you are the world's foremost expert on your own tastes.

Why bother, then, to learn to taste? One reason is that, for some people, discussing and analyzing a wine adds to the appreciation of it, just as studying the interplay of colors and forms can add to the enjoyment of a painting, or understanding principles of harmony can add to the enjoyment of a piece of music.

Another, more practical, reason is to become a more informed wine buyer. The more you understand about your own taste preferences, and the better you can describe them, the more likely you are to find a wine you like on a retail shelf or a restaurant wine list.

Identifying and describing the taste of a wine is simply a matter of experience, just like learning the tastes of other foods. Do you have a favorite type of apple? If so, how did you learn what it tastes like, and what distinguishes it from other apples? Probably by eating one and noticing that you liked its flavor best. How would you describe the taste, and how does it compare to other apples? Learning to taste wines involves answering the same kinds of questions.

Here are several learning strategies. It will help to have a source of many different wines, such as a wine merchant who is willing to listen to your tastes and make recommendations. (If your only source of wines is a supermarket or other self-service store, see the fifth chapter, "Wine &

Food," starting on page 59, for suggested food and wine combinations.) Learning about wines can be more fun and more informative if a number of people are involved. An informal dinner party is the ideal situation for a group of friends to enjoy food and wine and share their impressions as they learn more about wines. Many a "food and wine society" began as a series of monthly dinners and wine tastings, hosted by each member of the group in turn.

Start with your favorite dish. Ask your merchant to recommend a wine to go with it. Taste the wine by itself before dinner. Do you like it or not? Try to describe what you like or dislike about the wine. Then taste the wine with the dish. Does the taste of the wine change? Do the food and wine complement each other?

If you like the wine, get another bottle, plus a second wine of the same general type, and try them both with the dish a few days later. How does the second wine taste compared with the first? What do the two have in common? What makes them different? Does one taste better with the food than the other?

If you did not like the first wine, try to describe what you didn't like. Was it too sweet, too acid, too astringent (puckery), too high in alcohol? Does the wine leave any unpleasant sensations in your mouth, and if so, where? Describe the wine to your merchant and ask him or her to recommend another wine that you might like better.

Continue trying wines of the same type. Keep track of what all the wines have in common. After a while, you will have a general picture of what that variety of wine tastes like, and you will probably have found a favorite. You can then move on to a totally different type of food and another variety of wine. For instance, once you are familiar with Zinfandel and

its complementary foods, switch to a favorite seafood dish and ask for a recommendation for a white wine to go with it.

Start with a wine you like. Suppose you have found you like a certain brand of Riesling. Buy several bottles and try them with several different meals. See how the wine tastes with each different food. Do some foods bring out better flavors in the wine than others, or do some wines enhance the flavor of the food? Are some combinations unpleasant? Keep track of combinations that you like and try the same foods with other wines of the same type.

Pay attention to tasting terms used by others (see "Glossary of Tasting Terms," pages 44–45). These can come from many sources, such as the back labels on bottles, shelf tags or other descriptions in the store, descriptions of wines by wine writers in newspapers or magazines, or winery or retailer newsletters. Try the same wines and see if you can identify what is meant by each of the terms. (A word of caution, though—everyone's taste is unique, and just because some "expert" thinks a wine smells like black currants or tobacco or mint does not necessarily mean that you will find the same aromas.)

At a party where lots of different wines and foods are served, choose a wine you like and notice how it goes with various foods. Make a mental note of any especially good combinations, then try them again at home. Try the same foods with other wines of a similar type.

By following these tasting exercises, you will gradually build up a "library" of taste impressions in your memory. Each time you taste a new wine, you can compare it (consciously or not) to your memory of that type. At the same time, the new wine will become a part of your memory, too. Before long, you will become an expert on your own palate.

COMPARATIVE TASTINGS

In a sense, every wine tasting involves comparisons, either with wines tasted at the same time, or against the memory of others tasted in the past. We all have some taste memory of foods and wines we have had before. When we pick up an apple to take a bite, we already imagine its flavor, based on our experience with previous apples. Consciously or not, we judge each apple on whether it tastes like our general notion of an apple.

Tasting a wine by itself, we can compare it to our memory of other wines of the same type. But the easiest way to appreciate the sometimes subtle differences between one wine and the next is to taste several closely related wines together. The wines may be of the same grape variety, region, vintage, price range, or any combination of these.

Comparing several wines of the same variety and age (a "horizontal" tasting) is the best way to become familiar with that variety. By tasting what sorts of wine different winemakers have made with similar grapes, we can look for what they have in common as well as what makes each unique. For example, a horizontal tasting might be made up of 1970 Napa Valley Cabernets, 1981 Yakima Valley Rieslings, or 1983 Finger Lakes Chardonnays.

A "vertical" tasting is a comparison of several vintages of the same wine or of a closely related group of wines. Comparing wines from the same source (preferably the very same vineyards) gives a good picture of the differences in quality from one vintage to the next. Examples of vertical tastings could include Eyrie Vineyard Pinot Noirs from 1974 through 1980, or Heitz Cabernet Sauvignons from Martha's Vineyard and Bella Oaks Vineyard, vintages 1975, 1976, 1977, and 1978.

In competitive tastings, wines are usually judged "blind," that is, with

their identities concealed until after the wines are judged. This is done to prevent knowledge of the wine's identity from influencing a taster's opinion. Blind tastings are especially important when awards are at stake, or any time the wines must be judged completely objectively.

Comparative and competitive tastings have their pitfalls. First, they create the impression of winners and losers, but a wine that finishes in last place among a group of great wines may still be an excellent one. Second, there is a tendency to judge more harshly in a competitive tasting. Faults that would otherwise be overlooked take on major importance when one is trying to assign a ranking to basically similar wines. Perhaps most important, the wines are almost always judged without food. Some that are quite delicious at the table show rather poorly in tastings, especially against bigger, more assertive wines. Those that win the tastings may be less enjoyable at the table.

Gather friends for a horizontal tasting—a comparison of several wines of the same type and vintage. Being made from the same grape variety grown in the same year, the wines will show some similarities, but they will differ according to where they were grown and how they were fermented and aged.

GLOSSARY OF TASTING TERMS

Taste is an individual and personal matter. Although we all have the same sensory organs, no two people have exactly the same sensitivity to a given flavor or smell or color. Memory and experience play major roles in our subjective judgments. The result is that no one can say exactly how a wine will taste to another person. Still, there are times when we need to describe a wine, or to understand a description of one we have not tasted. The following is a set of standard tasting terms that are understood and shared by most wine professionals.

Acetic Having the odor or taste of acetic acid (vinegar). *Vinegary* is a less technical equivalent. Negative.

Acid, acidic A negative description, meaning too high in acidity.

Acidity A necessary flavor component in wines. Either too much or too little acidity is a fault; see *Flat, Sour, Acid, Tart.*

Aftertaste The overall taste and odor sensations remaining after the wine is swallowed. Some find this a negative term, preferring *finish.*

Alcohol The product of fermentation of sugar; anywhere from 7 to 20 percent of the wine by weight.

Alcoholic (adjective) Too high in alcohol for its type. Alcoholic wines often leave a "hot" feeling on the aftertaste.

Aroma The part of the odor of wine derived from the grape. *Fruity, flowery,* and *grassy* are names for aromas. Contrast with *Bouquet.*

Astringency The tactile sensation caused by tannin—a puckering, drying sensation, especially on the gums. Young red wines are often astringent, sometimes unpleasantly so.

Bitterness A flavor component of some wines, especially reds. Not to be confused with *acid* or *astringency.* Some bitterness comes from tannin and reduces with age. The degree of bitterness that is desirable is a matter of personal taste, but as an adjective, *bitter* has a negative connotation.

Body The "mouth-filling" quality of a wine. Basically a function of alcohol content, although sweetness can add body.

Bouquet The odors created by fermentation and aging, as opposed to *aroma,* which derives from the grape. Bouquet is harder to describe than aroma, but essential to the overall taste of wine, especially red.

Brilliant Used to describe wines of exceptional clarity. Positive. *Dull* and *hazy* are opposites.

Cloying Sweet and low in acid. Negative.

Complex Having many different flavor or odor elements. A desirable characteristic, the opposite of *simple.*

Corky, corked A moldy, spoiled odor from a contaminated cork; very rare with careful winemaking.

Dry Without any residual sugar. Wines that are not technically dry but with sugar levels below the tasting threshold (approximately 0.5 percent) may also be described as dry.

Finish See *Aftertaste.*

Flat Low in acid. This is said mainly of dry wines. See also *Cloying*.

Flavor The sum of the tastes, odors, and tactile sensations perceived by way of the mouth.

Flowery Having a pleasantly flowerlike aroma or flavor. Positive unless it is too pronounced.

Foxy The characteristic "table grape" or "grape jelly" aroma of many native American grapes, especially Concord grapes. It is liked by some, disliked by others.

Fruity Having the aroma and flavor of fresh grapes. Some may suggest other fruits, such as blackberries, apples, or currants. Fruitiness should be a component of all wines. A fruity wine need not be sweet.

Grassy The characteristic aroma of Sauvignon Blanc grapes. Positive unless it is too assertive.

Green Having the aroma of underripe grapes, usually accompanied by high acid and generally weak flavor.

Herbaceous A component of the aroma of certain grapes, especially Cabernet, Merlot, and Sauvignon Blanc. A positive quality in moderation; but see *Vegetal.*

Hot Unpleasantly high in alcohol. The term refers to a tactile sensation. Wines high in sulfur dioxide may also appear hot.

Hydrogen sulfide An odor like rotten eggs. Rarely found in carefully made wines; totally unacceptable.

Light Low in body. Can be positive, negative, or neutral, depending on the type of wine or the intended use.

Moldy The smell of wine made from moldy grapes; it is rare with careful winemaking.

Oaky See *Woody.*

Odor Anything sensed in the nose. A neutral word; there are good and bad odors.

Off odor A general term for all unpleasant odors in wine. With experience, the specific cause of the off odor can usually be named, but if it is really unpleasant, why bother?

Oxidized A sherrylike aroma caused by exposure of the wine to oxygen. It is desirable in sherry and Madeira types, but a sign of overlong aging or contamination with air in other types. Some tasters tolerate, even appreciate, a slight degree of oxidation in barrel-fermented or barrel-aged Chardonnays. Brownish colors are generally a sign of oxidation.

Raisiny   The aroma of overripe grapes, sometimes found in red wines. Zinfandels from warm growing regions often have a raisiny aroma. A little bit of it is tolerable in table wines, more is acceptable in port, but too much is a fault in any wine.

Simple   The opposite of *complex;* one-dimensional. Generally a neutral term; sometimes negative (when used for a wine that is typically complex), sometimes positive (as in "nouveau" red wines, which are released very young without any barrel aging).

Spicy   A component of the aroma of Gewürztraminer and some Muscat varieties, suggesting sweet spices. Can also be used to describe the black-pepper aroma of Petite Sirah and some Zinfandels.

Sulfur dioxide   The aroma of this gas (like the smell of a freshly struck match) is often felt as a painful prickle in the nose. Negative if detectable, although it evaporates quickly and the nose becomes accustomed to it almost as quickly.

Sweet   Having detectable residual sugar. Most tasters can detect 0.5 to 1 percent residual sugar. Table wines as sweet as 2 to 2.5 percent sugar can be pleasant with food, especially with enough acid to balance the sweetness; wines with higher sugar levels are generally considered dessert wines.

Tannic   High in tannin; see *Astringency*. Strong tea is a tannic liquid.

Tannin   An astringent substance extracted from grape seeds, stems, and skins during crushing and fermentation. Oak barrels also contain tannins that may be absorbed into the wine. A necessary part of wines that are to be aged, it diminishes with aging.

Tart   Relatively high in acidity, but more positive than *acid* or *sour*. Tart wines can be desirable, especially with rich or fatty-textured foods.

Thin   Lacking in body and flavor. In extreme cases the term *watery* may be used.

Vanilla   A component of the woody aroma, caused by vanillin absorbed from oak barrels.

Vegetal   A more extreme form of *herbaceous*. Tends to come from young vines in newly planted vineyards, especially in cooler areas.

Woody   Having a detectable odor or flavor of oak, from the barrels used to age the wine. Woodiness is caused by aging too long in oak barrels, especially new barrels. A slight touch of wood adds complexity to bouquet, but too much is undesirable.

Problem Words   Many commonly heard tasting terms actually mean entirely different things to different people. If you use them, be sure you know exactly what you mean.

Balanced   A very useful concept, it means that all elements (acidity, sugar or lack of it, body, aroma, bouquet) are in their proper proportions. However, some tasters use it to refer only to sugar-acid balance.

Big   Used by some tasters to mean only full-bodied, but by others to describe wines that are intensely flavored, tannic, or highly aromatic, or that combine some of these qualities.

Dry   Although this has a very specific meaning (the absence of sugar), many people use it in confusing ways. There are no degrees of dryness; a wine is either dry (with a sugar level below 0.5 percent) or it isn't. Calling a wine "dry, but not too dry" is nonsensical. Perhaps what many tasters mean by "too dry" is too high in acidity.

Full-bodied   As this term is commonly used (including its use in this book), it implies more than body; *full-flavored* is perhaps a more accurate term.

Hard   Variously used as a synonym for *tannic*, *acid*, or *hot*.

Harsh, rough, heavy, strong   Like *hard*, these words can refer to flavors or tactile sensations. The taster may know exactly what is meant, but others may not.

Musty   An ambiguous term for various off odors; it may or may not mean the same as moldy. Not related to *must*, the word for unfermented or partially fermented wine.

Soft   The opposite of *hard* in all its confusing meanings, *soft* can mean low in tannin, low in acid, or low in alcohol.

Sour   Commonly used to mean *acetic*, but experts frown on this usage. More or less the same as *acid*, in the sense of being too high in acidity.

Besides these terms, there is a whole range of subjective, even anthropomorphic, labels used by many wine tasters to describe the overall impression of a wine. These words have their uses in keeping track of one's own reaction to a wine; but when it comes to describing it to another person (say, a wine merchant who is trying to help find a substitute), they may be so too vague to be worthwhile. Some examples are: masculine, feminine, charming, generous, austere, voluptuous, stylish, aggressive, mellow, gentle, noble, well-bred, elegant, clumsy, awkward, nasty, powerful. Feel free to use them in your own tasting notes, but don't rely on them to communicate for you.

An underground wine cellar is the ideal place to store wine, but a cool closet in a city apartment can serve as a "cellar" for a few cases.

Storing & Serving Wine

O nce you've learned which wines you like and have begun to purchase a supply to have on hand, you'll want to store the bottles properly and serve them in the way that will show them off to best advantage. Some wines benefit from aging in the bottle; others do not. Some should be served chilled; others should not. In this chapter, you'll find guidelines for the best way to store and serve your wines, including information on wineglasses, corkscrews, breathing, and decanting.

STORING WINE

Wine, like other foods, must be stored properly to be kept at its best. It is not really perishable, like fresh fruit, but it does need a certain amount of attention to storage conditions to keep it from spoiling. And like other foods, wine should be served in such a way that it will show its best—at the right temperature and in an attractive glass.

In discussing how to store and serve table wines, it is useful to divide them into three categories: everyday, or "jug," wines; "great" wines; and the vast category between, which might be called "select" wines. The most common type throughout the wine-drinking world is the everyday sort: simple, straightforward wines consumed as a daily staple, like bread or dairy products. This category, which includes most American jug wines, makes a pleasant addition to the table but requires no special attention in storage or service. At the other end of the spectrum are the great wines: individual, excellent bottles that deserve to be handled carefully and served with a degree of ceremony and with carefully chosen foods. These wines are not, nor should they be, an everyday experience. Between these two extremes lies the large category of select wines. These wines complement foods very well; the wine and the food bring out nuances of flavor in each other, creating the kind of taste harmony that can make an ordinary meal a special occasion. Getting the most out of these wines requires some attention to storage and service.

BOTTLE AGING

When a bottle of wine leaves the winery, it is presumably ready to drink. However, some wines benefit from further aging in the bottle. The key word here is *some*. Most white wines will not improve in the bottle, and will, in fact, begin to deteriorate within a year or so of their release. The exceptions are oak-aged Chardonnays, which can improve for three to five years, and very sweet whites, which may be aged for a decade or more. The rest of the whites and almost all rosés should be drunk as young as possible to fully enjoy their fresh flavors.

In general, the best candidates for bottle aging are the fuller-bodied reds: Cabernet Sauvignon, Merlot, Zinfandel, and Petite Sirah. Aging these in the bottle continues the process that began in the barrel, softening the acids and tannin and giving more complexity to the flavor and bouquet. However, not all red wines should be aged; most Gamays, Zinfandels made in the lighter style, and some Pinot Noirs are most enjoyable in their fruity, zesty youth, and would only become dull and faded with further aging. Even some Cabernets are being made in a lighter, more "drinkable" style and are ready to drink at the time of their release.

Once you have decided to age a wine, the question becomes: How long should you let it age? After all, you cannot open a bottle, taste it, decide that it needs more age, cork it, and put it back in the cellar for another year. The only way to judge the aging potential of a wine is by experience.

To get an idea of the effects of aging, try this exercise: Find a young red wine that is available in quantity, such as a Cabernet Sauvignon or Zinfandel from the coastal counties of California. Taste a bottle and take notes on your impression of the wine.

If it has good body, good fruit, and a bit of tannin, then buy a case (12 bottles) and store them on their sides in a cool, dark place. Every three to six months, open another bottle and taste it, compare it to the memory of the last bottle, and record your impressions again. By the time you taste your way to the last bottle, you should have a feel for the effects of aging on that particular wine.

In general, the more body, acid, and tannin a wine contains, the longer it will take to become smooth and easy to drink. Once it has reached its peak, the wine goes into a sort of "plateau," during which it does not develop much, but remains at its best for drinking. With ideal storage conditions, the wine will remain in the plateau stage almost as many years as it took to get there; thus, a wine that begins to hit its stride when it is five years old will generally hold for another five years. However, even the biggest wine usually will begin to fade after a while, so beware of aging wines too long. If there is any doubt, it is better to drink a bottle too young, when it is still a little hard, than too old, when it is losing its charm.

Aging Guidelines

It is impossible to give aging guidelines for every type of wine; there is too much variation from one producer to the next and even from one vintage to the next. The following are overall ranges for each variety. Bigger, more tannic, higher-acid wines will tend toward the higher end of the range; wines that are lighter and more "approachable" when young will develop sooner. Cooler storage conditions slow down the aging process, while warmer or less stable temperatures cause wines to age more quickly. All figures are given as years after the vintage, which is in the fall: a 1984 wine will be only a little over a year old in the early months of 1986, but will be a full two years old by the fall.

Cabernet Sauvignon   Minimum three years, even in the lightest vintages. Fuller-bodied wines, such as the 1974, 1978, and 1980 vintages from Napa and Sonoma counties, need eight to ten years, and should last at least as many years longer.

Merlot   Usually matures a little faster than Cabernet, but most still need at least five years to show their best.

Zinfandel   Depends on the style. With high enough acidity and tannin, and no raisiny flavors, they can age just like Cabernets. But the simpler, fruitier style of Zinfandel is at its best two to five years after the vintage.

Petite Sirah   Five years minimum, although some are so tannic they may never be well balanced.

Pinot Noir   Four to eight years is a safe range, except for the lightest wines. Some of the more intense Pinots from mountain vineyards like Chalone and Mount Eden are still developing at ten years, but these are the exception.

Gamay Beaujolais   Not a wine for aging, especially if it is made in the nouveau style.

Chardonnay   Three to six years for the oak-aged types. Be careful not to age them too long; they may oxidize.

Late-Harvest Whites (Riesling, Gewürztraminer, Semillon, Sauvignon Blanc)   Three to five years of aging will improve most of these wines, even the ones with relatively low residual sugar (3 to 6 percent). The really sweet ones may last for decades, if you can wait that long.

Most other whites and almost all rosés should be bought as young as possible and drunk within a year after their release.

THE WINE CELLAR

Wine should be stored in a cool, dark, airy place with moderate humidity. The traditional place for such conditions is in an underground cellar, and over the years the term *cellar* has come to mean any place wines are stored. (The word is also sometimes used to mean the contents of the cellar—that is, the collection of wines.) A cool, dry section of a basement away from any source of heat, such as a furnace or water heater, is an ideal place to store wine. If your home doesn't have a basement, the bottom of a closet should work well. A garage is generally not a good place unless it is well insulated; most are too cold in winter or too warm in summer, or both.

Table wines and sparkling wines should be stored on their sides; this way the wine is always in contact with the cork, which keeps the cork from drying out. A cardboard wine

Wine bottles should be stored lying down, to keep the corks moist and tight, in a dark "cellar" with a constant cool temperature. The bottles should be left undisturbed until you are ready to serve the wine.

Above, a well-organized home cellar belonging to an avid wine collector. Bins made of boards set diagonally are ideal when you have several bottles or cases of the same wine. The lower section holds unopened cases of wine, stored with the corks down or on their sides. Note the thermometer (at left on the lower shelf) for keeping an eye on the cellar temperature. This cellar holds about twenty cases and is large enough to be used as a room for casual entertaining. Those with less space could adapt the system of shelves and bins to a smaller room, a single wall, or even a cool closet.

carton with dividers, set on its side, makes a simple holder for wine bottles. There are also many types of wine racks on the market. With racks or boxes, you can pull out one bottle without disturbing the rest, but if you expect to cellar many bottles of the same wine, a system of bins like the ones shown above makes better use of limited space.

A wine rack full of bottles may be an attractive bit of decor in your kitchen or dining room, but it really isn't the best way to store the wine. Wines "on display" are subject to bright light and fluctuating temperatures, both of which shorten the life of the wine. If you want to use such a rack, put in it only wines you will drink soon.

The ideal temperature for wine storage is between 55° F and 60° F. But a steady temperature is even more important. Any spot under 70° F will do, as long as the temperature does not vary more than a few degrees. Vibration is another enemy of wine, so try to locate your cellar away

from the refrigerator or other appliances with motors. Serious collectors may want to invest in a temperature-controlled wine cabinet. These self-contained refrigerated "cellars" maintain a constant 55° F, and hold anywhere from a hundred to over three hundred bottles. (Catalogs and information are available from America's Wineland Crafts, 680 Beach Street, Suite 349, San Francisco, CA 94109, phone 415-474-9000; or Kedco Wine Storage Systems, 475 Underhill Boulevard, Syosset, NY 11791, phone 516-921-3600.)

A refrigerator is not a good place to store wines for any length of time. Under refrigeration, corks will dry out faster than in a cellar and sparkling wines can eventually go flat.

Don't worry if your home does not have the ideal spot for a cellar. You can still age wines for a few years under the best conditions that you can manage and have the satisfaction of drinking more mature wines than you can currently buy.

SERVING WINE

It's always possible to pull a bottle of wine off a shelf, pour it into kitchen tumblers, and drink it as is. But attention to a number of details—the temperature of the wine, the proper glasses, a truly effective corkscrew, a method of chilling those wines that call for it, breathing and decanting where appropriate—will repay you with the greatest drinking pleasure each wine can afford.

Whether you are serving ordinary wines or great wines, serve them with pride. Don't apologize for serving modest wines, any more than you would for serving simple, home-style foods. On the other hand, don't let even the finest wine become a burden on you or your guests. Wine is to be enjoyed, not worshiped or analyzed or praised while the dinner gets cold.

SERVING TEMPERATURE

To show its best qualities, a wine should be served at the right temperature. The traditional rule is to serve white wines and rosés chilled, and red wines at room temperature. Like all rules, this one needs to be applied with some judgment.

There is a perfect temperature for every wine, ranging from thoroughly chilled (around 40° F) for sparkling wines and light, fruity whites to cool room temperature (65° F to 68° F) for the finest reds. The right temperature depends on the style of the wine; whether white, rosé, or red, the fuller-bodied, more complex wines need to be slightly warmer than the lighter, simpler wines.

Among the whites, sparkling wines are always best when served quite cold. A light, slightly sweet Chenin Blanc, Riesling, or hybrid wine is also at its most refreshing straight from the refrigerator. Whites with a more pronounced character, such as Sauvignon Blanc or Gewürztraminer, should be taken out of the refrigerator 10 or 15 minutes before serving to warm up slightly. A big oak-aged Chardonnay should only be chilled to about 50° F (30 minutes in the refrigerator or 15 minutes in an ice bucket will suffice), or its flavor will be dull. Very sweet whites, such as late-harvest Rieslings and Gewürztraminers, should also be served only slightly chilled to show off their ripe, luscious aromas. A few fine restaurants never refrigerate their best white wines and sparkling wines, but chill them to order and to the customer's taste.

Some wine lovers go to elaborate lengths to let red wines warm up to room temperature, even bringing the wine out of the cellar a day ahead of time. Unless your cellar is very cool, this is a waste of time and may even be a mistake. The rule of "red wine at room temperature" originated at least a hundred years ago, when most rooms were cooler than those of a modern American centrally heated home. It is important to remember that no red wine is going to be at its best above about 68° F. On a particularly warm summer day, or when your dining room is well heated against the winter chill, a fine Cabernet, Merlot, or Pinot Noir will taste best a few degrees cooler than room temperature. Lighter, simpler red wines are often best served straight from the cellar, or even lightly chilled in warm weather. Gamay is especially charming and refreshing after a quick dip in an ice bucket. Zinfandel that is made in a lighter, fruitier style should be served cooler than one made along the lines of a Cabernet.

If you are interested in precise measurement of the temperature of your wines, there are various types of thermometers available. A typical version uses a temperature-sensitive band that displays the temperature by lighting up a section of the band marked with the appropriate degrees. By strapping the band around a bottle, you get a temperature reading within a few seconds.

The ideal wineglass is simple and elegant in design, like the examples shown above. A glass with a large bowl is traditional for big red wines; the more delicate white wines are generally served in taller glasses with smaller bowls. Sparkling wines show their best in tall, slender glasses, such as the flute (fourth from left) or the elongated tulip shape (second from right). The small chimney glass (center foreground) is ideal for a 2- to 3-ounce serving of port, sherry, or other dessert wines.

GLASSES

After your own senses, a good glass is the most important wine-tasting tool. It is also an essential part of the enjoyment of wine at the table. The right kind of glass can enhance the appearance, aroma, and flavor of any wine. In fact, many wine regions of the world have developed distinctive styles of glassware to complement their wines. Here in America we can draw on the best designs the world has to offer to enjoy our native wines.

Everyday wines can be served in plain tumblers, as they are in many a home and café in Europe. Better wines deserve an attractive stemmed glass. The ideal wineglass is clear, with a stem long enough to be held without touching the bowl, and a generous bowl that either tapers inward or rises straight to a generous opening. The bowl should have a capacity of 9 to 16 ounces, so it can hold a 3- to 5-ounce serving of wine with plenty of room for the aroma to circulate in the glass.

Several specialized wineglasses are pictured above. Light, fruity white wines are often served in a tall glass with a small bowl; the long stem keeps the hand from warming the wine, and small servings stay colder. A big red wine will show its best qualities in a big glass, with plenty of room for swirling the wine to release its bouquet. The "chimney" glass, sometimes called a hurricane glass because of its resemblance to a hurricane lamp, is attractive and versatile and is made in a range of sizes. The smaller version is ideal for port, sherry, and other sweet or fortified wines, as well as for brandy.

Tall, slender "flutes" are perfect for sparkling wines; the small surface area keeps the bubbles in the wine longer than the familiar shallow glass does. Pouring the wine down the side of the glass rather than straight into the bottom will also keep more bubbles. Whichever glass design you use, do not fill the glasses to the brim, but leave some room at the top to allow the drinker to savor the aroma of the wine.

REMOVING THE CORK

To serve a bottle of wine, first you remove the top of the capsule (lead or foil wrapping), then you pull the cork. Removing the cork from a bottle of wine seems a simple enough proposition, but many people treat it as if it were some mysterious skill. With the right tool and just a bit of practice, it's easy.

All the devices available for pulling the cork can be divided into two categories: corkscrews, and everything else (see page 54). The simplest corkscrew is a coil of wire, pointed on one end and attached to a handle on the other. You screw it into the cork, give a yank, and the cork comes out.

Unfortunately, not every cork is willing to come out easily. As a result, corkscrews have been designed with every variety of leverage imaginable. The simplest is probably the double-wing model. After screwing it into the cork until the wings are pushed up and the body rests on the top of the bottle, you just press down on both wings to draw the cork up and out. The waiter's knife is a bit harder to master, but is a popular and reliable design; an arm attached to one end hooks onto the top of the bottle, and

the hinge forms the fulcrum. It also includes a small knife for cutting the capsule cleanly. (Incidentally, the finest corkscrews are distributed by the French Champagne houses. Why? When the top of a Champagne cork breaks, it takes an excellent corkscrew to get the rest out.)

Another type of corkscrew uses a second screw to pull the cork. Both the wooden model and the all-metal version rely on the same principle, but one screws a threaded tube out of the body, while the other screws a threaded handle down around a sliding tube, drawing the cork out with it. Both of these draw the cork smoothly and slowly without jostling the bottle, which is an important advantage in an older wine that has thrown a sediment.

Recently, a wine lover from Texas named Herbert Allen created the first real advance in corkscrew technology in almost two centuries, called the Screwpull. This ingeniously simple device uses a very long screw and a body to locate it on top of the bottle—nothing else. Pulling the cork is a simple matter: Align the body on top of the bottle, insert the tip of the screw, and turn. The screw goes down into the cork until the handle stops against the body, then as you continue turning, the cork climbs up the screw. There is now a pocket version of the Screwpull corkscrew complete with a knife for cutting capsules, which just might make all other corkscrews obsolete.

In choosing a corkscrew, be sure to look for one with a helical (open-centered) screw, rather than the type that looks like an oversized wood screw. The latter type bores a hole straight through the center of the cork, making it likelier that the screw will pull out of a stubborn cork.

CRYSTALS ON CORK

Occasionally, wine novices are startled to open a bottle of wine and find what looks like broken glass in the bottom of the bottle. It's not glass, merely harmless crystals of potassium bitartrate. During the wine-aging process, some of the natural tartaric acid in the wine precipitates (settles out of the wine) in the form of these tartrate crystals. Most of the tartrate deposits occur in the barrel or in storage tanks prior to bottling. (Wineries collect the crystals and sell them to food processors, who refine them into cream of tartar.) Sometimes, tartrates form in the bottle. If the bottles are stored standing on end, the crystals will form on the cork, as pictured above. Otherwise, they will sink to the bottom of the bottle. They are harmless, although they don't taste very good.

Another type of cork puller uses no screw at all, but two flexible metal blades that slip down between the cork and the neck of the bottle. You pull the cork by simultaneously twisting and pulling up. This device takes a little practice to master, and if used incorrectly it will neatly shove the cork into the bottle, but once mastered, it makes pulling the cork a fairly quick operation. A minor advantage of this tool is that you can reverse the cork-pulling procedure to recork the bottle.

There is one other type of cork extractor on the market—a long hollow needle attached to a compressed gas cylinder or a hand pump—but it cannot be recommended. The idea is to push the needle through the cork, then use the gas pressure to push the cork out. However, table wine bottles are not built to stand internal pressure, as sparkling wine or soda bottles are; it may never happen, but the possibly explosive combination of a weak bottle and a stubborn cork is frightening to contemplate.

Opening sparkling wines takes a special procedure. A loud pop, a flying cork, and wine foaming out of the bottle are all quite dramatic, but these are signs of bad technique. The cork can leave the bottle with enough velocity to injure someone, and even in "reentry" it can land in awkward places. Opening the bottle too suddenly also causes lots of the delightful and expensive bubbles to disappear before the wine gets to your guests' glasses.

There is a better (and safer) way to open sparkling wines. Start by tearing off the foil to expose the cork and wire. Pointing the bottle away from you and others, hold the bottle by the neck, with one thumb securely over the cork. Keeping your thumb firmly on the cork, undo the wire. If the cork is firmly in place, pull off the wire; but if the cork is beginning to ease out by itself, leave the wire in place. Grasp the cork (or the cork and the wire) firmly in one hand and the bottom of the bottle in the other. Holding the cork steady, twist the bottle off the cork. The cork should come out with a light pop, or maybe just a hiss of escaping gas. Now you can let go of the cork.

Ritual of the Cork: A Tableside Drama in Three Acts

Wine service in restaurants combines elements of tradition, good sense, and ostentatious foolishness. What should be a simple matter is often surrounded by so much showmanship and mystique that it can be intimidating to the diner. Still, there *are* a few essential steps that the restaurant should follow when you order a bottle of wine with your meal.

First, the unopened bottle is presented to the host of the party (or to the person who ordered it). A quick glance at the label will tell if it is the correct wine. If the vintage is different from that listed on the wine list, the waiter should volunteer that information.

Next, the waiter cuts the capsule with a neat cut on or below the raised portion of the neck. (Capsules are often made of lead, and the wine should not come in contact with the capsule in pouring.) If there is any deposit under the capsule, it should be wiped off before the cork is drawn. After pulling the cork, the waiter wipes the rim one more time to remove any trace of deposit, which might flavor the wine.

After inspecting and sniffing the cork for any signs of deterioration (which could mean a spoiled wine) the waiter places it on the table before the host. The host may choose to repeat the inspection; otherwise, the waiter pours an ounce or so of wine in the host's glass. The host

sniffs and tastes the wine, checking for any obvious faults and making sure it is at the right temperature. If all is well, the waiter pours each guest a moderate serving of wine, never filling glasses more than half full. The last step is to pour the host's portion, after which there should still be some wine left in the bottle for second servings.

If the wine is white, the bottle may be placed in an ice bucket to keep it well chilled. A red wine is placed on the table, preferably within reach of the host. Whether second helpings are poured by the waiter, the host, or the guests themselves depends on the formality of the restaurant.

This is the ideal situation. Unfortunately, some waiters (and some diners) do not understand the reasons for each step, and the result can be comical or downright aggravating. Of all the steps in the wine ritual, there is more nonsense over the cork than over any other aspect. Frequently, the host picks up the cork and sniffs it only because he or she has seen others do it. The process is often unnecessary, since many people have no idea what the cork "should" smell like and any fault in the wine will become obvious in the first taste. Inexperienced waiters sometimes wait for the customer to pass judgment on the cork, creating an awkward pause.

The host should taste and approve the wine before it is poured, but this is not the time for a careful analysis. The ritual of sniffing, pausing, sniffing again, taking a sip and slowly savoring the flavor and finish is fine at an analytic tasting, but here it just delays everyone else's enjoyment of the wine and the meal.

A few restaurants go in for decoration in the wine ritual. One of the silliest practices is tying a napkin around the neck of the bottle, which usually manages to do nothing but obscure the label. Even worse, some waiters carefully cut the capsule so that they can use it to tie the cork to the neck of the bottle. What this adds to the enjoyment of the wine is anybody's guess. Another misguided idea is to present the bottle reclining in a wine basket, a tool that has no place at the table, since it is intended only for decanting older wines.

Heavy-handed pouring is one of the most common problems in restaurants. A good waiter will fill each glass no more than half full, leaving some wine in the bottle for second servings. However, all too often the wine is poured generously, and the last of it is drained into the host's glass with the question, "Another bottle?" Invariably, at least one person at the table gets more wine than he or she wants, while another runs out before the meal is complete. Whether this happens by accident, inattention, or a deliberate attempt to sell more wine, it is a mark of inferior service.

An ice-water bath is the ideal way
to chill a fine sparkling wine.
What could be more
elegant or more appropriate
than a crystal ice bucket?

CHILLING THE WINE AND KEEPING IT COLD

Of the dozens of wine accessories, many are related to chilling a bottle of wine or keeping it chilled. The most basic of these is an ice bucket. An ice-water bath is the quickest way to chill a bottle and the most effective way to keep it cold. (Ice mixed with water in equal proportions is much more efficient than plain ice.) Ice buckets are available in crystal and silver, or in the less expensive stainless steel or polished aluminum versions sold by sparkling-wine distributors. Actually, any waterproof container large enough to hold a bottle at least halfway covered with ice and water will do for chilling, although only the more decorative ones should go to the table.

The disadvantage of an ice bucket is that the bottle, when it is extracted, is always dripping wet. Wrapping a napkin or towel around the bottle while you pour will catch most of the water. But there are also several "dry" methods of keeping a bottle cold. One is a cylinder of unglazed ceramic, just slightly larger than a bottle, which is soaked with water ahead of time; as the water evaporates, it cools the air around the bottle. Another is a double-walled cylinder of clear plastic that surrounds the bottle with an insulating layer of air. Even more effective are bottle holders that hold frozen inserts next to the bottle. For picnics, these ice-pack holders (or the even simpler foam-insulated bottle bags) will keep a refrigerated bottle at serving temperature for hours.

BREATHING AND DECANTING

Tradition holds that a red wine must "breathe," that is, it must be exposed to the air for some time before serving. But, as in the case of barrel aging, no two experts can agree precisely on how long it should breathe, or on what happens to the wine as it breathes. A whole range of chemical reactions begins when a wine is exposed to the air. Without getting too technical, these can be grouped into two types: oxidations (which occur when oxygen in the air changes certain components of the wine) and evaporation (which takes place when the volatile components of aroma and bouquet escape, either into the glass or into the air). Evaporation begins almost immediately and continues for hours, while oxidation is a slower process.

As these two sets of reactions occur, the wine is obviously changing. But is it getting better? Many expert tasters insist that red wines be allowed to breathe before tasting, and that all the wines in a comparative tasting breathe equally. Others claim that side-by-side comparisons of the same wine with and without breathing show no consistent pattern.

Young red wines seem to get the most benefit from breathing. An hour or two in the presence of air can give the impression of a slightly older, more complex wine, perhaps by speeding up some of the changes that occur in the bottle. But breathing any wine too long will leave it tasting flat and beginning to turn sour. Very old wines are best opened just before drinking, as they can begin to "fall apart" almost immediately.

Another reason for breathing wines is to remove flaws. An excess of sulfur dioxide, for example, will "breathe off" fairly quickly. A trace of the musty aroma of malolactic fermentation will also dissipate in a few minutes. But breathing will do nothing for other, more serious flaws, such as the presence of hydrogen sulfide or the smell of moldy fruit.

Whatever happens in breathing happens in proportion to the amount of wine in contact with the air. Very little can happen on the square inch or so of surface exposed in the neck of a full bottle. To get the best effects of breathing, the wine needs more air. The fastest way to achieve this is in a decanter or carafe. As the wine pours down the sides of the decanter, it has plenty of chance to absorb oxygen, just as swirling the wine in the tasting glass helps to open up its aroma. (In fact, more "breathing" probably goes on in the glass than anywhere else.)

Like most matters of taste, breathing wines is controversial. However, it's probably safe to say that an hour or two of breathing will not hurt most wines, though it is seldom necessary.

The decanter has another important use aside from allowing wines to breathe. Older wines, particularly reds, tend to form a deposit in the bottle. This sediment is harmless, but unpleasant to the taste and to the eye. A small amount of sediment can be dealt with by standing the bottle upright for a day or two before serving, then pouring carefully to leave it behind in the last bit of wine. Wines with a heavy sediment will need to be decanted.

If the bottle has been stored on its side, the sediment will form a thick line along one side. If possible, the bottle should be stood upright a day or two ahead to let the sediment fall to the bottom. Otherwise, the bottle may be cradled in a wine basket while the cork is drawn. In any case, handle the bottle gently so that the sediment is disturbed as little as possible. Place a light source (a candle is nice for this sort of ritual) next to the decanter to shine through the neck of the bottle. Pour the wine in a smooth motion into the decanter, watching the wine as it passes through the neck. Stop pouring when the sediment reaches the neck. If all goes well, you will only lose an ounce or so of wine, a reasonable price for the clarity and flavor of the rest.

Quickly cooked Veal Chops With Tarragon (see page 75) make a delicious foil for the subtle flavors of a Sonoma County Pinot Noir.

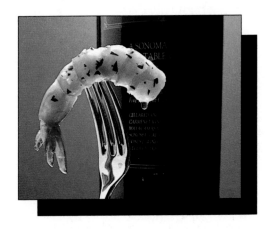

Wine & Food

One of the best places
to enjoy wine is at the
dining table. Even the
simplest wine can make some foods
taste better, and most wines taste better in
the company of food. When you find
the perfect combination of food and wine,
the sum is much greater than the parts.
This chapter explores the interaction of wine
and other good foods. Along with guidelines for serving wine with food, there is a
generous selection of recipes to try
with your favorite wines.

THE HARMONY OF FLAVORS

Over the years, countless writers and "experts" have put forth rules on which wines go with which foods. "Red wine with red meats, white wine with white meats" (including both fish and poultry) has been repeated so many times that the beginning wine drinker might think it was a commandment handed down from above. However, plenty of people enjoy food and wine combinations that go against these "rules." This chapter will explore the interaction of wine and other good foods and what makes certain combinations work.

Of course, such combinations are matters of personal taste. Some of the recommended pairings on the following pages are widely agreed upon, others are just one person's opinion. They are guidelines, not rules. Try them and see how they work for you, your family, and your guests.

Wine's greatest role at the table is as a flavor enhancer. A wine can accentuate certain flavors in foods, tame or soften others. Sometimes the wine echoes a flavor; at other times it offers balance or contrast. The food can act on the wine in the same way, highlighting some flavors and diminishing others. When the combination is right, both the food and wine taste better than either does alone.

Take, for example, a simple but delicious combination: a fruity wine with a touch of sweetness (say, a Riesling or a hybrid like Ravat) with ripe pears and a mild, creamy cheese such as a young Brie. The sweetness of the wine more or less matches the sweetness of the fruit, and the fruity aromas of the wine mingle with those of the pear. The acidity of the wine offers a refreshing balance to the combined sweetness of the fruit and the wine, and to the richness of the cheese, refreshing the taste buds ("cleansing the palate") before the next bite. Without the acidity of the wine, the cheese would seem a little duller and the pear simply sweet.

On the other hand, some combinations of food and wine are not so successful. Substitute oranges for the pears in the above example and the balance changes entirely. Oranges have so much acidity of their own that no wine can really balance it. The strong aroma of the oranges does not mix well with grape aromas either. Likewise, a very strong cheese would overwhelm the delicate sweetness of the wine.

The interplay of flavors and aromas can be compared to musical harmony. Similar flavors "resonate" like two notes played in unison. Complementary flavors "harmonize" like the notes in a pleasing chord. Some combinations create "dissonance" or harshness. Slightly sweet wine and sweet fruit sound the same note, but in different intensities; match them too closely, however, and they will fight, like two notes not quite at the same pitch. Sweet and acid, acid and rich, and sweet and rich are all harmonious, balancing combinations, and all three elements work together as well. Let one note sound too loud, however, and the harmony is destroyed.

Some of the most important interactions of food and wine involve flavors and textures not found in wine. Fat is a prime example. The acidity in wine decreases the tendency of fats to coat the tongue, thereby cleansing the palate between bites of fatty foods and keeping the senses fresh. Salty foods increase thirst, but in quenching thirst there is no major difference between wine and other liquids. Pungent or "hot" flavors, such as pepper, ginger, and capsicum (chile peppers), react differently with different components of the wine. Alcohol can accentuate hot flavors (perhaps because of the "hot" sensation of the alcohol itself), but the sugar in sweet wines diminishes the effect of hot ingredients (see "Problem Foods," page 78).

WHICH WINE WITH WHICH FOOD?

Like wine tasting, food-and-wine tasting can be as simple or as complicated as you wish. You may find that one or two wines are a suitable accompaniment to all sorts of foods. After all, millions of people drink the same wine every day. In much of the countryside of Europe, there is one local wine, most of which is consumed within a few miles of where it is grown. Most of this everyday wine is red, but that fact doesn't stop people from enjoying it with fish or fowl as well as meat and cheese. The same thing happens in white-wine regions; the everyday wine is white, and it is served with everything.

It was in the cities of Europe, rather than in the wine country, that the traditions of serving certain wines with certain foods began. The well-to-do inhabitants of Paris, London, Brussels, and other cities had the luxury of sampling wines from all over the continent with foods from all over the world. In the process, they discovered some particularly good combinations, such as Champagne with oysters, and port with Stilton cheese.

American wine drinkers have an equally wide range of wines from which to choose. Finding the perfect foods to match each wine and choosing wines to enhance the flavor of certain foods can be an enjoyable lifelong pursuit. Beware, however, of taking it too seriously; remember that wine is meant to add pleasure, not work, to your meals.

In choosing a wine and food to go together, consider what you are trying to accomplish. Are you trying to come up with a wine to complement a special dish, or vice versa? Do you plan to serve one course or several, one wine or several? Consider the guests. Are they wine lovers, or do they just have a glass now and then? Do you plan to pay a lot of attention to the food and wine combinations, or just enjoy the meal without particular emphasis on its elements?

In most cases, you choose the menu first, then the wine or combination of wines to go with it. Maybe crab has just come into season, or you want to fix Uncle Harry's favorite dish, or you just feel like having chicken tonight. In any case, you would probably choose a wine that you know goes well with the dish you are preparing.

There may be times, however, when you want to serve a particular bottle of wine. It might be someone's favorite, a gift bottle, or something new that you want to try. In that case, the menu should be planned with the wine in mind. This is especially true when serving great wines, but it really applies to all good wines.

If you will be serving more than three or four people, you will probably want to have more than one bottle of wine. You could serve two bottles of the same wine, but why not take advantage of the opportunity to try two different wines? In this way, you'll double the chances that everyone at the table will find a wine and food combination that they enjoy.

The choice of wine depends somewhat on your guests. Naturally, you want to offer the best you can, regardless of whom you are serving, but try to keep your guests' wishes in mind. If you know Uncle Harry thinks all dry wines taste like vinegar, you are not doing him a favor by serving a great bottle of dry wine, no matter how good you think it is or how "right" it is with your menu. He would probably be happier with a sweeter one. If the occasion is a reunion of family or old friends who have not seen one another in a long time, the dinner-table conversation is not likely to focus on subtle differences between two fine Chardonnays. Rather than trying to turn the meal into a tasting, just serve a selection of good wines that fit your menu.

WINE WITH APPETIZERS AND SOUPS

A first course of soup or an appetizer not only gives variety and balance to a menu, but it may suggest a different wine as well. A fish soup makes a nice prelude to a main course of beef or lamb; but don't expect the same wine to complement both dishes.

Following the general principle of serving lighter wines before heavier ones, most people prefer to serve a white wine at the beginning of a meal. Sparkling wines are often an ideal choice both before dinner and with the first course.

In a traditional menu of several courses, dry sherry is often served with the soup. It is certainly a good combination, especially with bean soups, but many people prefer a dry table wine instead. Creamed soups call for a wine with some richness, but enough acidity to balance the creamy texture of the soup; most Chardonnays fit the bill, as do the fuller-bodied Sauvignon Blancs.

Some vegetables, such as asparagus or artichoke, can give a quite pronounced flavor to soups. Serving an assertive wine like Sauvignon Blanc with such soups could be a mistake, as the flavors would fight. A better choice would be a milder wine—a dry Chenin Blanc, a French Colombard, or a nice brut.

Appetizers, whether served at the table or during a "cocktail hour," should not be too spicy. The stuffed mushroom caps at right can go with almost any wine, white or red. The Spicy Meatballs With Peanut Sauce on page 62 are about as highly seasoned an appetizer as you would want to serve with wine; try them with a slightly sweet wine, such as a Gewürztraminer or Riesling, or an extra-dry sparkling wine.

MUSHROOM CAPS WITH CHICKEN-LIVER STUFFING

12 large mushrooms (see Note)
   Oil for sautéing
2 chicken livers
2 green onions, minced
1 or 2 cloves garlic, minced
½ teaspoon grated fresh ginger
2 tablespoons chopped parsley
2 to 3 tablespoons fine bread crumbs
2 tablespoons grated Asiago or other Parmesan-type cheese
   Salt and freshly ground pepper to taste

1. Preheat broiler. Choose large, good-looking mushrooms with caps that are still closed or just beginning to open.

2. Hold each mushroom by the cap and bend back the stem. It should snap off where it joins the cap. Combine stems and any broken caps and chop very finely with a knife or in a food processor.

3. Heat oil in a skillet over medium heat. Roughly chop the livers and cook them in the oil until firm, but not fully cooked. Remove livers from pan. Add green onion, garlic, ginger, parsley, and chopped mushroom stems to the pan. Cook over high heat until the liquid exuded by the mushrooms is nearly gone. Stir in bread crumbs and remove the pan from the heat. Meanwhile, chop livers very finely, almost to a paste.

4. Season mushroom mixture to taste with salt and pepper. Combine it with the chopped chicken liver and stuff the mushroom caps with this mixture. Broil until the stuffing is lightly browned, about 5 minutes. Allow to cool slightly before serving.

Serves 3 to 4 as an appetizer.

<u>Note</u> Buy more mushrooms than the number you plan to serve, because some will undoubtedly break when you remove the stems.

BLACK BEAN SOUP

This soup is traditionally served with dry sherry, sometimes with a spoonful of sherry stirred in at serving time. Some of the bigger Chardonnays, especially those with more than 13 percent alcohol (such as Belvedere, Conn Creek, or Sanford) could stand in for the sherry very nicely.

- 1 *pound black turtle beans (about 2½ cups)*
- 1 *ham hock or ham bone, or ¼ pound smoked pork neck bones*
- 1 *medium onion, chopped*
- 1 *dried chile pod, seeds and veins removed, or 1 table-spoon mild chili powder*
- ½ *teaspoon ground cumin*
- 1 *bay leaf*
  Salt and freshly ground black pepper to taste
- ½ *cup sour cream (optional)*
- ¼ *cup sliced green onion or chives (optional)*

1. Pick over beans carefully. Place beans in a large, deep pan with the ham hock or bones and cover with water by at least an inch. Add onion, chile, cumin, and bay leaf. Bring to a boil, reduce heat, and simmer, covered, until the beans are tender, about 2½ hours. Check soup from time to time to make sure the beans are still covered with water; add boiling water if necessary.

2. Remove ham hock and let it cool enough to handle. Cut meat off the bone, shred it finely, and set aside. Discard skin and bones.

3. Purée soup in a blender, food processor, or food mill. Return soup to pot, add shredded meat, and season to taste. If soup is too thick, thin with stock rather than water. Simmer 15 minutes or so before serving.

4. Lightly beat sour cream (if used) to a smooth consistency. Swirl a little sour cream into the center of each bowl and top with a sprinkling of green onion or chives.

Serves 6.

SPICY MEATBALLS WITH PEANUT SAUCE

Try these as an appetizer with sparkling wine, Sauvignon Blanc, or dry Gewürztraminer.

- 1 *pound lean boneless pork*
- 2 *teaspoons chopped fresh ginger*
- 2 *large cloves garlic*
- ½ *teaspoon ground coriander*
- ¼ *teaspoon ground cumin*
- ¼ *teaspoon ground black pepper*
- 1½ *teaspoons fish sauce or soy sauce*
- ¼ *teaspoon salt*
  Oil for sautéing

Peanut Sauce

- 2 *tablespoons oil*
- 2 *tablespoons each chopped garlic, ginger, and green onion*
- ¼ *teaspoon hot pepper flakes*
- 2 *tablespoons sugar*
- ¼ *cup each soy sauce and water*
- ½ *cup peanut butter*
- ¼ *cup chopped cilantro*

1. Cut pork into 1-inch cubes. Chop ginger and garlic together in a food processor, then add pork, coriander, cumin, pepper, fish sauce, and salt. Process in 2- or 3-second pulses until the meat is finely chopped and the mixture clumps together. (The mixture can also be ground finely in a meat grinder or finely chopped by hand.)

2. Form meat mixture into 1-inch meatballs and chill until ready to cook. (Meatballs may be prepared several hours ahead.)

3. Heat oil in a large, heavy skillet and sauté the meatballs over medium heat until evenly browned and cooked through, about 10 minutes. Serve hot as an appetizer, with cocktail forks or toothpicks for dipping in Peanut Sauce.

Makes 2 dozen meatballs.

Peanut Sauce Heat oil in a nonstick skillet and sauté garlic, ginger, green onion, and hot pepper. Dissolve sugar in soy sauce and water and add to pan. Stir in peanut butter and cilantro. Serve warm or cold. Can be made a day ahead.

FOUR CORN SOUPS

Sweet yellow corn makes an attractive flavor and color background for all sorts of soups. Here are four examples based on a single recipe; you can doubtless come up with more. The base of all four soups is the same: a partially puréed mixture of corn kernels, green onions, and milk. Rich, flavorful white wines are best with these soups, although a Pinot Noir can be surprisingly good with the red pepper and smoked fish versions—the sweet richness of the corn seems to bring out a sort of sweetness in the wine, even though it is dry.

CORN AND RED PEPPER SOUP

- 4 *ears fresh corn, husks and silk removed*
- 4 *medium green onions*
- 3 *tablespoons butter*
- 1 *large red bell pepper or fresh pimiento, diced*
- 3 *cups milk or half milk and half chicken stock*
  Salt and freshly ground pepper to taste

1. Working over a bowl, hold each ear of corn by the stalk and cut the kernels off the ears with a small, sharp knife. Do not cut too close to the cob; the idea is to slice off only the top two thirds of each kernel. With the dull side of the blade, scrape the cob thoroughly to squeeze all the juice out of the bases of the kernels. Purée half the corn in a food processor or food mill and return it to the bowl. Slice the white and pale green parts of the green onions, reserving some of the green tops for garnish.

2. Heat butter in a large saucepan. Add green onion and pepper, and cook over moderate heat until soft but not brown. Add corn, stir and cook 2 minutes, and add the milk. Bring soup just to a boil, reduce heat, and simmer 10 minutes. Season to taste and serve, garnished with chopped green onion tops.

Serves 6.

Corn and Shrimp Soup Omit the red peppers from the basic recipe. Substitute ¼ pound raw shrimp, peeled and roughly chopped. Serve with a light Chardonnay or a dry Riesling or Gewürztraminer.

Corn and Green Chile Soup Substitute 1 or 2 mild green chiles, roasted and peeled, for the red pepper. Garnish the soup with cilantro leaves and serve it with a grassy Sauvignon Blanc.

Corn and Smoked Fish Soup Substitute ¼ pound boneless smoked trout, albacore, or black cod, diced or shredded, for the red peppers. Serve with a rich Chardonnay.

The three corn soups shown here illustrate how a change in ingredients can suggest a change in the accompanying wine. The basic version (at left), made with red peppers, calls for a rich Chardonnay or Pinot Noir. Replace the peppers with green chiles (at right), and the more assertive flavor of Sauvignon Blanc is a better match. With shrimp or other shellfish (at top), a light, fruity Riesling or Gewürztraminer with good acidity would be best.

Fish and shellfish are generally served with white wines, but aromatic Red-Wine Seafood Stew made with Zinfandel goes well with a glass of the same wine.

WINE AND SEAFOOD

White wine is usually recommended with fish and shellfish. Yet many seafood dishes are delicious with red and rosé wines. Millions of people who drink red wines every day of their lives would not think of switching to white wine just because seafood is on the menu.

There are good reasons why white wines are generally recommended with seafood. Many types of fish and shellfish are delicate in flavor, so a lighter wine offers a better balance. Wines with high acidity (which includes most whites) cut through any "fishy" flavors better than low-acid wines. Fish does not get along with tannic wines as well as red meats do, and some tasters (though by no means all) find that the combination of red wine and fish accentuates the fishy taste or produces an unpleasant metallic taste. These are all matters of personal taste; let your experience be your guide.

Sweet wines are not usually recommended with seafood, although you might find that a slightly sweet wine goes well with the sweet flavor of certain shellfish, especially scallops, shrimp, and lobster. More likely, though, the two sweet flavors will clash, and a drier wine would provide a better balance.

Most blanc de noirs and rosé wines will go well with seafood, as long as they are not too sweet. Among reds, serve lighter, fruitier wines with good acidity and little tannin: Gamays, Pinot Noirs, or lighter, nontannic Zinfandels and Cabernets.

☐ Oysters and Champagne are a classic combination, and with good reason. The rich texture of raw oysters would be too much to bear without the refreshing acidity of the wine, which sets up the palate for the next oyster. Brut or natural sparkling wines are best, but other light, dry white wines are also suitable. This is not the place for a big, rich Chardonnay or an oak-aged Sauvignon Blanc, although both would go well with a creamy oyster stew.

☐ Simple steamed, poached, or broiled fish, especially the leaner varieties, should be served with lighter wines that will not overpower the flavor of the fish: a dry Chenin Blanc, light Chardonnay, or Semillon.

☐ Fish with more complicated sauces can take more assertive wines: a Sauvignon Blanc or Gewürztraminer goes well with strong herbs, ginger, or garlic, and an oak-aged Chardonnay is a nice complement to creamy sauces.

☐ Freshwater fish, especially trout, go particularly well with dry Riesling.

☐ Tuna, swordfish, or salmon steaks grilled over charcoal can go very nicely with a medium-bodied Zinfandel or Cabernet.

SHELLFISH BISQUE

A lot of the flavor of shrimp, crab, crayfish, and lobster typically gets thrown away with the heads and shells. The frugal cook, however, can make a delicious dish out of a small amount of fresh shellfish and a batch of frozen shells and heads. If you buy shrimp in the shell or pick the meat from your own crabs, by all means save the shells in the freezer. With a bag of frozen shells, you can cut the amount of fresh shellfish in the following recipe in half.

Serve this soup with your favorite shellfish wine—a Sauvignon Blanc, perhaps, or a middle-of-the-road Chardonnay.

> 1½ pounds shrimp (preferably with heads on), crab, crayfish, or lobster
> 1 tablespoon packaged Shrimp Boil, Crab Boil, or Old Bay seasoning mix
> ¼ cup butter
> 1 medium onion, diced
> ½ cup diced celery
> 1 bay leaf
> 1 sprig fresh thyme
> ½ teaspoon paprika
>   Pinch cayenne pepper
> 3 cups extra-rich milk or half-and-half
>   Salt and freshly ground pepper to taste

1. If using live shellfish, boil or "steam" them in water seasoned with the packaged spice mix. (Allow 5 to 7 minutes for crayfish or blue crabs, a little longer for Dungeness crab or lobster. They are done when the shells turn bright red or orange.) If using frozen shellfish, poach it in the seasoned water until the meat is opaque. Let the shellfish cool and reserve the liquid.

2. Remove meat from shells, chop it finely, and set it aside. Chop shells and heads with a knife or in a food processor, being careful to include all the tasty fat inside.

3. Heat butter in a large saucepan over medium heat. Add onion and celery and cook until soft but not brown. Add chopped heads and shells, bay leaf, thyme, paprika, cayenne, and about ½ cup of the reserved cooking liquid. Cook 15 minutes and strain through a fine-mesh strainer into a bowl or another saucepan. Discard the shells and the vegetables.

4. Combine strained stock, milk, and reserved chopped meat and bring to a simmer. Cook at a simmer (do not boil) just until the meat is heated through (cooked through if you are using raw shrimp), correct the seasoning, and serve.

Serves 4.

RED-WINE SEAFOOD STEW

This is probably the best introduction to the combination of red wine and seafood. Serve it with the same type of wine used in the stew, or with a dry rosé made from the same variety. In warm weather, you might want to serve the wine slightly chilled.

> 2 pounds fish heads and bones (preferably a lean white fish—rock cod, sea bass, snapper, flounder, halibut)
> 1 bunch green onions
> 1 large fennel bulb (also sold as sweet anise)
>   Half a bottle dry red wine (Cabernet or Zinfandel)
> 1½ cups water
> 1 pound tomatoes, peeled, seeded, and chopped
>   Pinch saffron or 1 teaspoon Mexican safflower threads
> 1 bay leaf
> 1 teaspoon cracked peppercorns
> 2 tablespoons olive oil
> 18 mussels, scrubbed and debearded
> 2 tablespoons chopped garlic
> 1½ pounds fillet of mild white fish (see list above), in ½-inch cubes
> 1 pound squid, cleaned, sacs flattened and cut into strips

1. Clean fish heads and bones thoroughly, removing the gills (if present) and any traces of blood or organs. Split the heads if large. Place the heads and bones in a nonaluminum stockpot.

2. Trim green tops and roots from green onions. Roughly chop the trimmings and add them to the stockpot. Trim the green tops from the fennel bulb and add ½ cup of these trimmings to the pot. Add wine, water, half the tomatoes, saffron, bay leaf, and peppercorns. Bring to a boil, reduce heat, and simmer 30 to 45 minutes.

3. While stock is simmering, trim the root end from the fennel bulb, split bulb in half lengthwise, and slice crosswise into ¼-inch slices. Slice green onions into ½-inch sections and set them aside with the tomatoes.

4. Strain finished stock through a fine-mesh strainer. Heat oil in a heavy, 8-quart, covered saucepan or casserole over moderate heat. Add sliced fennel, cook for a minute or two in the oil, then add about ½ cup of stock. Cover and let fennel steam until just tender, about 7 to 8 minutes.

5. Add mussels, garlic, and remaining tomatoes to pan. Cover, bring to a boil, and steam until the mussels open, about 6 minutes. Add the remaining stock and fish, and simmer until the fish is opaque, 3 to 5 minutes, depending on the density of the fish. Add the squid to cook for the last minute.

6. Serve in shallow bowls with crusty French bread. Add hot-pepper sauce to taste, if desired.

Serves 6 as a main course, 8 or more as a first course.

STEAMED SALMON WITH TARRAGON

This dish works best with a delicately flavored salmon. If you are using Pacific king or silver salmon, plan to make it early in the spring or late in the fall, when the fish are a little leaner and milder in flavor than they are in midsummer. Farm-raised Norwegian salmon, which is flown here fresh almost all year, is also ideal for this treatment. Serve with a lighter-style Chardonnay or a dry Chenin Blanc. Snow peas stir-fried with sliced water chestnuts make a good side dish.

To steam the fish, you will need a large covered pot with a rack to hold a plate a few inches above the boiling water. A wok with a steaming rack is ideal for this number of servings. For a larger piece of salmon, to serve six or more people, you will need a large oval roasting pan with a cover. *Caution:* Steam can cause severe burns. Always open the steaming pot away from you, and for the most protection for your wrists and forearms, wear long sleeves and long oven mitts.

- 2 green onions, sliced
- 1 salmon fillet (1 in. thick; 1 to 1½ lbs)
- 2 tablespoons dry white wine
- ¼ teaspoon salt
- ⅛ teaspoon freshly ground white pepper
- 1 tablespoon fresh tarragon leaves

1. Choose a decorative heatproof plate that will fit into the steaming vessel. Scatter the green onions over the bottom of the plate. Lay salmon fillet over green onions, skin side down, folding the tail section under, if necessary to fit the plate. Sprinkle salmon with the wine, then with the salt and pepper, and finally with the tarragon leaves.

2. Bring water in steamer to a rolling boil. Remove the cover, opening it away from you to let the steam dissipate a little, then place the plate on the steaming rack. Cover and cook until the center of the fish is just done, about 10 minutes.

3. Serve the fish from the platter, spooning a little of the liquid from the plate over the top of each serving.

Serves 4.

OYSTER STEW WITH RED-PEPPER BUTTER

This creamy stew is a perfect foil for a rich Chardonnay with a good backbone of acidity, such as Chateau St. Jean, Edna Valley, or Acacia.

- 2 tablespoons softened butter
- ½ teaspoon sweet paprika
  Pinch cayenne pepper
- 1 pint small, shucked oysters, with their liquor
- 3 cups milk
- 1 cup whipping cream

1. In a small bowl beat butter until light and fluffy. Beat in the paprika and cayenne and set aside for at least 1 hour to allow the flavors to ripen.

2. Drain oysters well, reserving the liquor. Combine liquor, milk, and cream in a saucepan over medium heat. Bring mixture almost to a boil, reduce to a simmer, and add oysters. Cook until oysters are plump and the edges begin to curl.

3. Ladle the stew into shallow bowls. Put a dollop of the red-pepper butter in the middle of each bowl and let it melt into the stew.

Serves 4.

WINE AND POULTRY

Poultry is wine's most versatile partner. The mild flavor of poultry forms an agreeable background to so many ingredients that it can be matched with just about any wine. The preparation of the bird, and the accompanying ingredients, thus determine the choice of wine.

In the familiar scheme, poultry is "white meat" and is generally served with white wines. To show a great white wine in its best light, serve it with a boneless breast of chicken (there's one on page 101). Chilled white wines are also the ideal accompaniment to cold poultry dishes and barbecued chicken. But red wines certainly have their place with poultry. In fact, many wine drinkers prefer a red wine with most birds. A simple roast chicken is one of the best dishes to show off a good red wine, and the fuller flavors of duck, goose, and game birds practically demand a full-bodied red.

Coq au vin, or chicken with wine, is a perfect example of the versatility of poultry. While we usually associate the name with the Burgundian version made with red wine, any dry wine will work. An interesting exercise is to make coq au vin with a different variety of wine each time—such as Riesling, Sauvignon Blanc, Zinfandel, and Cabernet—and serve the same variety of wine to accompany the dish. You might find some combinations that surprise you.

Often, the ingredients combined with the poultry in a dish can best determine the choice of wine. Dominant herbs like tarragon and rosemary suggest herbaceous wines, especially Sauvignon Blanc, Cabernet Sauvignon, and Merlot. Wild or dried mushrooms call for deeply flavored wines—Zinfandel and Petite Sirah among reds, Chardonnay or Pinot Blanc if a white is desired. Fruit-flavored sauces or stuffings taste best with a lighter, fruitier Gamay, Pinot Noir, Chenin Blanc, or Riesling.

GALLINA EN MOLE
Chicken in spicy sauce

To match the complex flavors and textures of this Mexican-inspired sauce, choose a soft, round red wine—Pinot Noir, Gamay, or aged Merlot or Zinfandel.

- 2 *tablespoons chicken fat or oil*
- 4 *pounds chicken parts*
- 4 *cloves garlic, peeled*
- ¼ *cup chopped onion or shallot*
- 1½ *cups chicken stock*
- ¼ *cup chopped raisins or prunes*
- ¼ *cup roughly chopped almonds*
- 2 *tablespoons powdered California or New Mexico chile (see Note)*
- ½ *teaspoon ground cinnamon*
- ¼ *teaspoon each ground allspice and anise seed*
- 2 *tablespoons masa harina (tortilla flour) or finely ground white cornmeal*
- 2 *tablespoons peanut butter or sesame tahini*
- 1 *teaspoon salt*
- 1 *ounce unsweetened chocolate*

1. Heat fat in a large, covered casserole over moderate heat. Brown chicken pieces a few at a time. Pour out fat, add garlic and onion, return chicken pieces to the pot, and add ½ cup of the stock. Cover and braise until chicken is tender, about 45 minutes.

2. Meanwhile, assemble the other ingredients. Combine raisins and almonds in one dish. Combine chile powder, cinnamon, allspice, anise, and masa harina in another. If you have a spice grinder, grind them all together with the masa.

3. When chicken is done, transfer to a plate and keep warm. Pour braising stock into a bowl and let the fat rise to the surface. (Can be prepared to this point several hours ahead.)

4. Skim 2 tablespoons fat from the braising stock and return to pan. (Any remaining fat can be discarded.) Heat fat over medium-high heat.

Sauté raisins and almonds until almonds just begin to color, but do not let them burn. Stir in spice mixture and cook a few minutes until fragrant. Add peanut butter, the reserved braising stock, and the remaining 1 cup stock. Add salt and bring sauce to a simmer.

5. The sauce can be served as is, but for a smoother sauce, transfer the sauce to a blender or food processor and purée to a smooth consistency. This may have to be done in batches; if you overfill the jar, the sauce could overflow and scald you.

6. Crumble chocolate and stir it into sauce. Taste sauce and correct the seasoning. Return chicken to sauce to reheat. Serve with rice.

Serves 4 to 6.

<u>Note</u> Be sure to use pure chile powder, not the prepared spice mixture sold as chili powder. California chile is milder, New Mexico a little hotter.

Gallina en Mole is adapted from the classic Mexican mole poblano, a rich stew of turkey or chicken in a complex sauce of ground chiles, spices, nuts, seeds, and a little chocolate. Here, the chiles are toned down considerably to blend better with wine.

Special Feature

WINES FOR THANKSGIVING DINNER

According to Leon Adams in *The Wines of America*, the Pilgrim settlers of Plymouth, Massachusetts, made wine from the wild grapes growing near their colony, so wine was presumably served at the first Thanksgiving dinner. Wine is no less appropriate today as an accompaniment to the harvest celebration. However, with the wide choice of wines now available, deciding which wines to serve with this most traditional American meal is much more complicated than it was for the Pilgrims.

Most poultry can be served with either white or red wines, and roast turkey is no exception. The choice of wine for the holiday table has more to do with the rest of the menu. If your taste runs to sweet side dishes such as candied yams, stuffing with fruit, and cranberry sauces or relish, then a young, fruity, perhaps slightly sweet wine is in order. Gewürztraminer is the favorite "turkey wine" in many families, but Riesling or White Zinfandel would also be a good choice. Among the reds, a Gamay or Zinfandel made in a lighter style goes best with this type of menu. November is also the prime season for nouveau-style wines, and with their

straightforward fruity flavors, these wines are delicious and refreshing with holiday meals.

If you prefer to serve more "serious" wines with your Thanksgiving meal, try one of the better Pinot Noirs, a richer Chardonnay or Pinot Blanc, or a well-aged Cabernet or Merlot. In this case, you may want to adjust the menu slightly, playing down the sweet dishes and placing more emphasis on nutty flavors such as wild rice, chestnuts, and baked squashes.

Of course, a nice bottle of brut or natural sparkling wine is always a good accompaniment to appetizers, and there's no reason not to serve the same wine throughout your holiday meal if you like.

CHICKEN PIE WITH OLIVES

Try this Moroccan-style dish with Cabernet or Merlot and see how the green-olive aromas of the wine mingle with the olive-scented chicken.

    2½ pounds chicken parts (legs,
        wings, gizzard, and heart of
        one fryer, for example)
        Salt and pepper
     2 tablespoons olive oil
    10 cloves garlic, peeled
     1 medium onion, diced
     ¼ cup each finely diced carrot
        and celery
     1 cup Cabernet or Merlot
     1 bay leaf
     1 sprig fresh thyme or
        ½ teaspoon dried
     ⅓ cup roughly chopped Kalama-
        ta or other Greek-style olives
     3 eggs
     ¼ cup chopped parsley
     1 teaspoon fresh thyme leaves
        (optional)
     1 partially baked 9-inch
        unsweetened pie shell

1. Season chicken lightly with salt and pepper. Heat oil in a covered flameproof casserole over medium heat. Brown chicken pieces; remove from pan. Add garlic, onion, carrot, and celery; cook until onion is translucent but not browned. Return chicken to pan; add wine, bay leaf, thyme, and olives. Bring to a boil, reduce heat, cover, and simmer until meat is falling off bones, about 45 minutes.

2. Preheat oven to 350° F. Remove chicken from pan. Bring sauce to a boil and reduce by two thirds. When chicken is cool enough to handle, discard skin and remove meat from bones. Cut meat into small cubes; add to sauce. Taste chicken mixture for seasoning; correct if necessary.

3. Beat eggs with parsley and thyme until slightly frothy. Spread chicken mixture in pie shell. Pour eggs over top. Cover pie with foil; bake 20 minutes. Remove foil; bake until top is browned, 10 to 15 minutes more.

4. Serve in wedges, hot or warm.

Serves 4 to 6.

WILD RICE AND RYE STUFFING WITH PRUNES

Chef Richard Alexei of Monticello Cellars in the Napa Valley makes a delicious poultry stuffing of wild rice and whole rye grains, which are generally available in natural foods stores. This version, adapted from his recipe, also includes prunes, and is especially good with Pinot Noir.

     1 tablespoon each butter and
        oil or chicken fat
     ¼ cup wild rice
     ½ cup whole rye grains
     1 medium onion, diced
     6 pitted prunes, diced
     2 cloves garlic, minced
     ½ cup dry white wine
     2 cups chicken stock or broth
     ½ teaspoon salt (omit if using
        canned chicken broth)
     ¼ teaspoon dried thyme
        Salt and freshly ground
        pepper to taste
        Liver or other giblets,
        cooked (optional)
     1 beaten egg

1. In a large, heavy saucepan over medium heat, heat butter and oil. Add wild rice and rye and cook, stirring frequently, until slightly browned and fragrant. Stir in onion, prunes, and garlic and cook 3 to 4 minutes more.

2. Add wine, stock, salt, and thyme and bring to a boil. Reduce to a simmer, cover, and cook until grains are tender, about 1 hour. Check liquid partway through the cooking; if grains become dry before they are tender, add water or stock as needed; if mixture is too wet, remove cover and boil it down.

3. Season stuffing with salt and pepper. If you are using giblets, dice them; add to stuffing. Stir in egg.

4. Let stuffing cool before putting it into the bird. *Note:* The stuffing may be made a day or two ahead and refrigerated, but do not stuff the bird until just before roasting.

Makes enough stuffing for a 4- to 5-pound chicken or duck. Double or triple the recipe for a turkey.

LOCAL WINES WITH LOCAL FOODS

One of the best bits of advice given to those traveling in Europe is to seek out local food specialties and drink local wines. Generally, they complement one another nicely. Which came first is hard to tell, but it is safe to say that they "grew up together." Whether consciously or not, the cooks make dishes that taste good with the local wine, and the winemakers make their wines to appeal to the local taste. Over the centuries, a strong bond has usually formed between regional foods and wines.

Here in America, we have not had that much time to evolve local food and wine affinities. Nevertheless, there is a certain appeal to drinking a Chardonnay from Oregon's Willamette Valley or a Yakima Valley Riesling with fresh Pacific salmon, a Sauvignon Blanc from California's Sonoma County with Sonoma goat cheese, New York State Baco Noir with local Cheddar, or white wines from Virginia or Maryland with Chesapeake Bay blue crab.

Preserving and promoting regional food specialties is a topic of growing interest. At the same time, more and more places in the United States are making fine wines. As a result, travelers here may also do well to try the local foods with the local wines.

TWO MEALS FROM
TWO DUCKS

Cutting up a duck into parts allows much more flexibility in cooking methods and menu planning than trying to deal with the whole bird. The following menus show how to make two delicious meals from a pair of ducks.

The choice of wine for these two menus depends partly on the food, partly on the company. The first menu calls for a more "serious" wine, while the second is for a less formal situation such as a group of friends invited for Sunday dinner, and the wine should be just as familiar and comfortable.

MENU I

DUCK DINNER
FOR THE BOSS

Olives and Toasted Nuts

Dry Sherry

*Grilled Duck Breasts With
Red Onion Sauce*

Rice Pilaf With Duck Livers

Steamed Asparagus

*Robert Mondavi or Stag's
Leap Cabernet Sauvignon*

*Raspberry Sherbet
and Cookies*

Coffee

This menu is an impressive meal for company that can be put together in less than an hour using boneless duck breasts. The duck livers go into a delicious pilaf to accompany the duck breasts (although it really deserves to be served on its own as a first course). A prestigious Cabernet or Merlot is in order here.

MENU II

DUCK DINNER
FOR OLD FRIENDS

Crudités

Duck Stewed in Red Wine

Polenta

Steamed Cabbage Wedges

Fruit and Cheese

*Pedroncelli or Fetzer
Zinfandel*

After making grilled duck breasts for a fancy company meal, use the rest of the ducks to make this rich, satisfying stew, inspired by a pair of recipes in Paula Wolfert's The Cooking of South-West France. *This dish is meant to be enjoyed in comfortable clothes with comfortable friends. Invite your guests into the kitchen to nibble on the crudités while you put the finishing touches on the stew. A modest Zinfandel, a hybrid red, or even a good jug red goes well with this menu.*

GRILLED DUCK BREASTS WITH RED ONION SAUCE

1 pound red or yellow onions
2 tablespoons duck or chicken fat or olive oil
1 cup dry red wine
1 teaspoon honey, or more or less to taste
1 sprig fresh thyme
1 bay leaf
2 whole duck breasts, skinned, boned, and split
Salt and freshly ground pepper

1. Peel the onions and slice them as thinly as possible (a food processor fitted with a 2mm slicing blade does this well).

2. Heat fat or oil in a heavy saucepan over medium heat. Add onions and cook, stirring frequently, until they begin to wilt. Adjust the heat so that the onions do not brown.

3. Add wine, honey, thyme, and bay leaf. Bring to a boil, reduce to a simmer, and cook until the onions are quite soft, about 20 minutes.

4. Taste the sauce; it should be slightly sweet, but balanced by the acidity of the wine. Adjust with honey or vinegar as needed; cook another 5 minutes. Keep sauce warm.

5. Season the duck breasts and grill or broil them to the medium-rare stage, 3 to 4 minutes per side. Serve the breasts on top of the onion sauce.

Serves 4.

RICE PILAF WITH DUCK LIVERS

2 tablespoons butter or oil
1 cup long-grain rice
1 tablespoon minced shallot or onion
2 cups well-seasoned chicken stock
Pinch dried thyme or sage
2 duck livers

1. In a medium skillet heat the butter. Add the rice and shallot and sauté until the rice is thoroughly coated with oil.

2. Add chicken stock and thyme. Bring to a boil, cover, and simmer until all the liquid is absorbed, about 25 minutes. Dice the duck livers and stir in for the last 5 minutes of cooking.

Serves 4.

Medium-rare Grilled Duck Breasts with a sweet-tart Red Onion Sauce make an elegant entrée that can be prepared in less than an hour. Rice Pilaf made with the duck livers can be served as a first course or as a side dish.

DUCK STEWED IN RED WINE

Don't be dismayed by the number of steps in this recipe; this is a meal that can be prepared over the space of several days. You can make the stock (steps 1–3) the first day, braise the duck (steps 4–5) the same day or the next day, and hold the dish in the refrigerator for several days before finally reheating and serving it. Like most stews, the flavor improves with a few days' aging.

> *Legs, wings, necks, giblets, and carcasses of 2 ducks*
> *1 onion, roughly chopped*
> *½ cup each diced carrot and celery*
> *2 cups unsalted chicken stock*
> *Half a bottle dry, full-bodied red wine*
> *3 sprigs parsley*
> *1 sprig fresh thyme*
> *1 bay leaf*
> *½ teaspoon cracked black peppercorns*
> *2 tablespoons flour*
> *Salt and freshly ground pepper to taste*
> *¼ cup minced shallot*

1. *The first day:* Preheat oven to 400° F. Remove excess fat from the legs. Skin necks and cut them into 2-inch lengths. Remove the tips from the wings. Set legs, neck pieces, giblets, and trimmed wings aside in the refrigerator.

2. Remove all skin and fat from the carcass. The skin and fat can be rendered to provide an excellent cooking fat for other dishes; otherwise, discard it. You are now left with the skinned carcass and wing tips of the two ducks. With a heavy knife or cleaver, chop each carcass into half a dozen pieces. Scatter the pieces in a roasting pan with the onion, carrot, and celery, and roast until nicely browned, about 30 minutes.

3. Transfer roasted duck bones and vegetables to a stockpot or large saucepan. Pour chicken stock and wine into roasting pan and stir to deglaze, then add to stockpot. Add parsley, thyme, bay leaf, and pepper. Bring stock to a boil, reduce heat, and simmer 45 minutes to 1 hour. Strain finished stock and discard the bones and vegetables. (Recipe may be completed to this point a day ahead of braising the duck, several days ahead of serving.)

4. Combine flour, salt, and pepper. Dredge duck pieces in flour; shake off the excess. Heat oil or fat in a large ovenproof casserole and brown duck pieces well, a few at a time, removing them when they are browned.

5. When all duck pieces have been removed, scatter in shallot, add stock, and bring to a simmer, stirring to loosen any bits of flour stuck to the pan. Dice giblets and add them to sauce. Return duck pieces to sauce, cover, and cook over low heat or in a 250° F oven until duck is tender, about 1 hour. Let stew cool uncovered, then refrigerate overnight.

6. *On serving day:* Preheat oven to 250° F. Remove and discard all fat from surface of stew. Bake stew until meat is thoroughly reheated, about 1 hour. Skim off any remaining fat, taste, and correct seasoning if necessary. Serve over polenta or slices of hearty bread.

Serves 4.

STEAMED CABBAGE WEDGES

> *1 head cabbage*

1. Trim any battered outside leaves from cabbage. Cut it in half lengthwise; cut each half into wedges, each including part of core. Steam until just tender, 5 to 8 minutes.

2. Transfer wedges to a cutting board, cut away core, and transfer intact to plates (slide knife blade under wedge to lift it in one piece).

Serves 4 to 8, depending on size.

WINE AND RED MEATS

"Red wine with red meats, white wine with white meats" has always been the rule, but like all rules, it has its exceptions. True, most people enjoy a red wine with beef, lamb, and game, but there are those who like the combination of a big Chardonnay with rare roast beef. Who is to say they are wrong? Veal, and to a lesser extent pork, are generally said to go with white wines, but most dishes of either could go with red or white.

Beef, with its rich flavor and generally high fat content, calls for a wine with plenty of flavor and acidity. The same richness also softens the effect of tannin, making a young red seem more mature and drinkable. But which red wine? The debate over which wine best complements a plain grilled steak may go on forever. Some prefer the soft and supple flavors of Pinot Noir, others the strength and complexity and "backbone" of Cabernet, and still others the forthright fruitiness of Zinfandel. Each of these wines has something to offer, but it is hard to say which is best.

Cold beef, and other cold meats for that matter, go well with a whole range of wines, from full-bodied whites to dry rosés and lighter reds.

The more pronounced flavor of lamb, which goes so well with robust herbs and garlic, makes either Zinfandel or Cabernet the wine of choice. Syrah and Petite Sirah are also good choices with most lamb dishes.

Fresh (rather than cured) pork can be served with either red or white wine, depending on the accompanying ingredients. A roast loin stuffed with prunes brings to mind a Pinot Noir, charcoal-grilled chops with rosemary or sage a young Zinfandel, braised pork with cabbage a dry Gewürztraminer, and medallions sautéed with apples and cream a fruity Chardonnay. Sausages are best with a not-too-serious red wine (or, of course, with beer). Ham is tricky to match with wine, especially if the cure is very sweet, but the best solution is either Gewürztraminer or a nouveau-style Gamay.

The term *veal* covers quite a range in this country, from the true milk-fed veal of the East and Midwest to the more mature meat raised in the West. The mild, white eastern variety goes very well with Chardonnay and other dry whites, but the western variety is dark enough and beefy enough in flavor that it should be treated like beef.

Domestic rabbit is as versatile as chicken, which it resembles somewhat in flavor, and can be served with the same wines. Wild rabbit or hare is stronger in flavor, and calls for the stronger flavor of red wine.

SAUTÉED BEEF STEAKS MARCHAND DE VIN

This simple dish, "wine merchant style," relies on two basic ingredients: good beef and good red wine.

> 1½ to 2 pounds tender beef steaks (filet, strip, sirloin) ¾ to 1 inch thick
> Salt and freshly ground pepper
> 2 tablespoons minced shallot
> ½ cup red wine
> 4 tablespoons butter

1. Heat a heavy skillet over medium-high heat. Rub skillet with a piece of fat trimmed from the steak. Cook steaks, turning once and seasoning after turning with salt and pepper, to the desired degree of doneness.

Test for doneness by pushing on the steak with your finger: A rare steak just begins to offer resistance; at the medium-rare stage, it springs back lightly; cooked to medium or beyond, it gets increasingly stiff and resistant to the touch. Remove the steaks to warm plates.

2. Add shallot to pan and cook in the meat juices until translucent. Add a little of the butter if the pan is nearly dry. Add the wine, bring to a boil, and reduce by two thirds. Remove pan from heat, swirl in butter, check the seasoning, and spoon the sauce over the steaks.

Serves 4.

Sautéed Beef Steaks Marchand de Vin is a beef-and-red-wine-lover's dream dish—tender, aged beef and a deglazing sauce of good red wine, enriched at the last minute with a bit of butter.

Rack of lamb, an international favorite, makes a perfect combination with Zinfandel, strictly an American wine.

RACK OF LAMB WITH HERBS

Rosemary, oregano, thyme, and bay leaf, either alone or in combination, are delicious with lamb. The garlic- and herb-flavored salt rub in this recipe could easily be adapted to other cuts of lamb, such as a roast leg of lamb or a boned and rolled shoulder.

> 1 rack of lamb, 2 to 2½ pounds (see Note)
> 2 or 3 cloves garlic, peeled and thinly sliced
> 2 tablespoons fresh herbs (see list above) or 1 teaspoon dried
> 1 teaspoon kosher salt
> ¼ teaspoon freshly ground pepper

1. Preheat oven to 450° F. Remove excess fat from lamb. With the tip of a knife, make several shallow incisions in the meat and remaining fat, and push a slice of garlic into each cut. If you are using fresh herbs, chop them finely together with any remaining garlic. If you are using dried herbs, crumble them finely.

2. Combine herbs, salt, and pepper. Rub this mixture on all sides of the lamb. Place lamb, fat side up, on a rack in a roasting pan.

3. Place lamb in oven, reduce heat to 400° F, and roast (without basting) to desired degree of doneness, about 25 minutes for medium rare (internal temperature 140° F). Allow lamb to rest, loosely covered with foil, at least 10 minutes before serving. Carve into chops to serve.

Serves 2 to 4 (2 or 3 chops each).

<u>Note</u> For easier carving, have the butcher cut through the backbone between the ribs. After roasting, the rack can then be neatly carved into single-rib chops.

VEAL CHOPS WITH TARRAGON

If pale pink milk-fed eastern veal is available in your area, by all means try this simple but elegant treatment. Serve with a fine full-bodied Chardonnay, such as Far Niente, Shafer, or Mountain House. The redder, beefier-tasting veal typical of the West can be prepared the same way, but tastes better with a lighter red wine, say a Pinot Noir or Gamay.

> 4 veal rib chops, ¾ to
>   1 inch thick
> 2 or 3 sprigs fresh tarragon
>   (see Note)
> 1 teaspoon kosher salt
> ¼ teaspoon freshly ground
>   pepper
> ½ cup unsalted chicken, veal,
>   or beef stock or ¼ cup canned
>   stock mixed with ¼ cup water

1. Trim excess fat from chops. Finely chop half the tarragon and combine it with the salt and pepper. Rub salt mixture all over both sides of chops.

2. Heat a large skillet (nonstick or well-seasoned cast iron) over medium heat. Add chops; cook until center springs back readily when pressed with a fingertip, 3 to 4 minutes per side. Remove chops to a warm platter or to individual plates.

3. Deglaze skillet with stock, scraping up any browned drippings. Add remaining tarragon leaves. Reduce sauce by half, taste for seasoning, and correct if necessary.

4. Spoon sauce over chops, decorating each with tarragon leaves.

Serves 4.

Note If fresh tarragon is not available, use 1 teaspoon crumbled dried tarragon leaves to season the chops and omit the extra tarragon from the sauce. Or use tarragon leaves packed in vinegar (available at specialty shops), well drained, in place of the fresh leaves.

BRAISED OXTAILS À LA CHINOISE

Oxtails make a particularly rich, satisfying stew. They can be substituted in the braised beef recipe on page 98, but try this delicious East-West treatment. Serve with Pinot Noir or another soft, round red wine.

> 2 tablespoons oil
> 1 oxtail (about 1¼ pounds),
>   cut into 2-inch lengths
> 1 large onion, diced
> 1 carrot, peeled and diced
> 1 cup slightly sweet Riesling
>   or Chenin Blanc
> 2 tablespoons soy sauce
> 3 or 4 slices fresh ginger
> 1 strip (2 in.) orange or tangerine rind, white pith removed
> 1 whole pod star anise (available in Chinese groceries or
>   spice shops)
> ½ teaspoon pepper

1. Heat oil in a heavy, covered casserole over medium heat. Pat oxtails dry, then brown evenly, removing them from pan as they brown.

2. Add onion and carrot to pan and cook 2 to 3 minutes, without browning. Add wine and soy sauce, bring to a boil, and stir to scrape drippings from bottom of pan.

3. Reduce heat to a simmer. Return oxtails to pan. Add ginger, orange rind, star anise, and pepper, cover and cook over lowest possible flame until tender, about 3 hours. Skim off and discard excess fat. Taste for seasoning and correct if necessary.

4. Serve with sauce and vegetables, alone or over noodles. (Recipe may be made ahead and refrigerated 2 to 3 days before serving.)

Serves 2 to 3.

WINE AND CHEESE

Like wine, cheese is an ancient food that goes back to the earliest days of agriculture. It is not surprising, then, that wine and cheese go together very well. There is probably not a wine that cannot be matched to one cheese or another, nor a single cheese that cannot be served with some wine. But some combinations of wine and cheese go together better than others.

The basic rule is to serve full-flavored cheeses with full-flavored wines, milder cheeses with lighter wines. Red wines generally fare better with cheese than do white wines, but there are plenty of exceptions. A few cheeses (Limburger, for example, or fully ripe Liederkranz) are so strong that no wine can really stand up to them; if you decide to serve a wine with these, your best choice is a pleasant, light white wine. If you want to show a fine wine in its best light, serve milder cheeses that allow the subtleties of the wine to come through.

Though it may be possible to name a "best" wine for every cheese, it is easier to match wines to related groups of cheeses, such as the following.

Fresh cheeses, such as cream cheese, pot cheese, and ricotta, are the mildest in flavor. They are usually combined with more flavorful cheeses or with other foods such as smoked salmon. As a result, the choice of wine usually depends on the other flavorings.

Soft-ripened, white-rind cheeses like Brie and Camembert can go with a wide range of wines. When very young and mild (while the rind is still snowy white or cream colored), they go well with dry whites or even slightly sweet wines. As the cheeses mature and the rind becomes streaked with a rusty hue, switch to a softer red wine, especially Pinot Noir or Gamay.

Port, blue cheese, autumn fruits, and walnuts—a perfect four-way marriage of flavors, and one that tastes especially good on a chilly evening.

Stronger soft or semisoft cheeses generally call for red wines. Italian Fontina, with its deep, rich, nutty flavor, goes best with an equally full-flavored wine: a bigger-style Pinot Noir, Merlot, mature Cabernet Sauvignon, or Zinfandel. This same type of wine is also a safe bet with most of the dozens of varieties of soft and semisoft French cheeses, such as Port-Salut, Saint-Paulin, Reblochon, and Saint-Nectaire.

The Swiss cheeses, including Gruyère, Emmenthaler, Norwegian Jarlsberg, and Danish Samso, as well as domestic Swiss, go well with most wines, but particularly with the lighter-style Chardonnays and the lighter, fruitier reds. The best French Gruyère types, generally sold as Beaufort or Comté, call for a more "serious" red, such as those recommended for Fontina above.

Cheddar cheeses from England and North America (and the somewhat similar French Cantal) are particularly nice with Cabernet and Merlot; something about the firm texture and relatively high fat content of the cheese softens the taste of tannins in a younger Cabernet. An even better combination to many people is a well-aged Cheddar with ruby port and walnuts.

Soft-ripened, washed-rind cheeses, such as Pont l'Evêque, Muenster, Esrom, and Liederkranz, can be too strong for a wine with much subtlety. Lighter, fruitier wines are in order—nouveau-style reds or white Zinfandel, for example. In Alsace, Gewürztraminer is a traditional accompaniment to Muenster.

Milder semisoft cheeses, such as Bel Paese, Edam, Havarti, Danish or Swedish Fontina, and Monterey jack, are among the most agreeable cheeses with a wide range of wines. Almost any red wine, and most dry whites, will go well with these cheeses.

Hard cheeses of the Parmesan type are usually thought of just as grating and cooking cheeses, but finer examples of this type can also be served by themselves. The original and finest of the type, the Italian Reggiano Parmigiano, can be served with the best aged red wines. The same goes for a really old Gouda, which can be just as hard as a Parmesan. Most of the others of the type, including many Italian imports as well as domestic Parmesan and Asiago, are a little sweeter than Reggiano, and go better with a young and fruity wine, either red or white.

AN AMERICAN WINE AND CHEESE BUFFET

Rouge et Noir Brie or Camembert (California)

Sonoma Jack (California)

New York or Vermont Aged Cheddar

California Chèvre

Maytag Blue (Iowa)

Aged Asiago (Wisconsin)

Assorted Breads and Crackers

Apples, Grapes, or Pears

Green Olives, Toasted Almonds, Gherkins

Crudités

Yakima Valley Riesling (Washington)

Central Coast Chardonnay (California)
or
Finger Lakes Seyval Blanc (New York)

Willamette Valley Pinot Noir (Oregon)
or
Sonoma or Napa Valley Gamay (California)

Amador County or Paso Robles Zinfandel (California)
or
Albemarle County Cabernet Sauvignon (Virginia)

This menu is an example of an American-style cheese and wine buffet, a selection of regional wines and cheeses from all over the United States. Of course, you could also choose an international selection of cheeses, and you can always add or subtract cheeses and wines according to your taste.

ENTERTAINING WITH WINE AND CHEESE

A wine and cheese buffet can make excellent party fare, as long as you avoid the commonplace "Cheddar, Swiss, and Brie, burgundy and chablis." A good cheese board can consist of as few as three or four cheeses, or a dozen or more, depending on the number of guests. The key is to provide a variety of flavors and textures. Wines should also be chosen for variety, so that at least one wine will suit every guest's taste.

Here are some pointers on assembling a selection of wines and cheeses:

☐ For a party at which dinner will not be served, allow about ¼ pound of cheese per person and one bottle of wine for every three or four guests. Allow half as much for a before-dinner "cocktail hour." (Remember, cheese is filling; don't overdo it before dinner.)

☐ The number of cheeses and wines depends in part on the number of guests. Don't spread the selection too thin; it's better to have an ample supply of a few than to have a dozen of each but run out of half of them in the first ten minutes.

☐ Try for a balanced selection of cheeses by choosing one example from each category. A good selection to begin with is one soft-ripening cheese (Brie, Camembert), one semisoft cheese (Port-Salut, Monterey jack), one firm cheese, either of the Swiss or Cheddar type, and one blue-veined cheese. With more guests, add a stronger soft or semisoft cheese (Pont l'Evêque, Esrom), a hard cheese (Parmesan, aged Gouda), a goats'-milk cheese, a double- or triple-cream cheese (Boursault, Saint-André), an herbed or spiced cheese (Cumminost, Havarti with dill), or whatever other types you like.

☐ Follow the same approach with the wines. Start with one dry red, say a Zinfandel or a lighter-style Cabernet, and one slightly sweet white, such as Chenin Blanc or Riesling. Next, add a dry white (Chardonnay or Sauvignon Blanc) and a different style of red (such as Gamay Beaujolais). Unless the purpose of the party is to provide an opportunity for tasting as many wines as possible with a variety of cheeses, keep the wine selection simple.

☐ Serve an assortment of breads or crackers with the cheeses. Avoid highly seasoned crackers if you want the flavor of the cheese and wine to come through. With really fine cheeses, thin, unsalted crackers or matzos are best.

☐ Other nice accompaniments to a cheese board are crunchy raw vegetables (celery, carrots, cucumbers, cauliflower, broccoli, radishes), nuts, olives, and fresh fruits, especially apples and grapes. Some guests might also enjoy a few condiments like chutney, gherkins, and fancy mustards.

☐ To show cheeses at their best, serve them at room temperature. Provide plenty of knives or cheese slicers, at least one for each cheese, to facilitate serving.

PROBLEM FOODS

Not all foods go well with wine. Vinegar and chiles are two obvious examples, and some would add anchovies to the list. Because their flavors are strong and concentrated, they do not harmonize well with wine. Combining a noticeably vinegary dish (such as a salad dressing) with a wine of normal acidity creates too much acid to begin with; in addition, the different acid flavors fight with one another. Similarly, the heat of fresh or dried chiles can combine with the hot sensation of the alcohol in the wine, increasing the fire rather than putting it out.

Just because a dish contains vinegar or chile does not mean, however, that you cannot serve wine with it. The key is moderation. If you use lots of vinegar and a neutral oil in salad dressing, no wine is going to taste good alongside it. On the other hand, if you use a good olive oil to supply the flavor and just a bit of vinegar—or, better still, lemon juice—there is no reason to put aside your wineglass.

Highly seasoned foods made with fresh or dried chiles are not easy to match with wines. After all, chile, ginger, cardamom, and the like are not native to wine-growing regions. Lighter, more refreshing beverages work best—fruit juices, beer, or coconut-based drinks, for instance. If you want a wine to complement highly seasoned dishes, stick to fruity whites, well chilled, with perhaps a bit of sweetness.

Cuisines in which wines are not usually served are likely to have some dishes that lend themselves better than others to a wine accompaniment. The Mexican menu on page 84, the Southeast Asian buffet menu on page 82, and the Chinese menu on page 89 are examples.

Blue cheeses may seem too strong to go with any wine, but lots of people enjoy Roquefort or Gorgonzola with a full-flavored red wine. Others prefer a sweet wine, such as a late-harvest Sauvignon Blanc or Riesling. Stilton and port form a classic combination, as any lover of either will confirm.

Goats' milk cheeses do not always follow the above rules. Some people find their distinctive flavor unsuited to red wines, but marvelous when matched with the herbaceous flavors of Sauvignon Blanc. It is certainly a combination that works, but a young and fruity Zinfandel also makes a fine complement to goat cheeses.

Serving Wine and Cheese

In a traditional menu of many courses, the cheese comes toward the end of the meal, just before the dessert. Some people prefer to skip the dessert and finish with the cheese course. Either way, a piece of cheese is a nice accompaniment to whatever wine is left from the main course. Add a piece of ripe fruit and you may decide you don't need that slice of Triple Chocolate Indulgence.

If you want to make a more elaborate course of the cheese, choose two or three different varieties, perhaps one each from the categories listed on the preceding pages. If the wine served with the main course doesn't particularly match the cheeses you want to serve, feel free to bring out another wine that will. Examples of menus that include a cheese course are on pages 70 and 84.

SWISS FONDUE WITH GEWÜRZTRAMINER

A simmering pot of cheese fondue is a delightful dish for casual entertaining. Each diner spears a cube of bread on a long fork, then swirls it in the communal pot to coat it thoroughly with the cheese mixture. These bite-sized morsels can then be eaten directly from the fork, washed down with the same sort of wine that went into the pot.

A dry or slightly sweet Gewürztraminer is an unconventional ingredient for a classic Swiss fondue, but it works. The combination of cheeses is traditional, but you can also use Jarlsberg or even a mild Havarti. If you prefer to serve a red wine, try a light, fruity Gamay, but use a white wine in the fondue itself.

Half a loaf stale French bread
1 cup Gewürztraminer
1 clove garlic
½ pound each Gruyère and Emmenthaler cheese, grated
2 tablespoons flour
Pinch ground nutmeg
Salt and freshly ground pepper to taste

1. Cut bread into 1-inch cubes and set it aside to dry out slightly.

2. In a fondue pot or chafing dish, bring wine to a boil with garlic. Meanwhile, grate cheese on a coarse grater. Toss grated cheese in flour to coat it lightly and evenly.

3. When wine comes to a boil, discard garlic clove and stir in cheese and nutmeg. Cook, stirring frequently, until all the cheese is melted and the mixture begins to thicken. Season to taste with salt and pepper.

4. Transfer the pot to a heated stand on the table. Adjust the heat so the cheese mixture barely simmers. Spear cubes of bread on long forks and swirl them in the cheese.

Serves 3 to 4.

BLUE CHEESE SOUFFLÉ

This makes an elegant first course; served with a salad and fruit and cheese for dessert, it can also be the main dish for a light supper. Real French Roquefort is the best cheese to use, but the excellent Maytag Blue from Iowa makes a very good second choice. Serve with a lighter-style Cabernet Sauvignon.

The recipe is easily expandable to up to twice the proportions given, as long as you have a baking dish large enough to contain the soufflé. Allow a little more baking time for larger soufflés.

- 2 tablespoons finely grated Parmesan cheese
- 2½ tablespoons butter
- 3 tablespoons flour
- 1 cup milk
- 3 ounces blue cheese, crumbled Pinch ground nutmeg Salt and freshly ground pepper to taste
- 4 egg yolks
- 6 egg whites, at room temperature

1. Preheat oven to 400° F. Choose a soufflé dish or other deep baking dish of about 6-cup capacity. Rub the inside of the dish with a little butter, add the grated cheese, and roll the cheese around to evenly coat the bottom and sides of the dish.

2. Melt butter in a heavy saucepan over moderate heat. Stir in flour and cook until flour turns a pale tan. Stir in milk and cook until sauce is thick, stirring frequently to break up any lumps. Add blue cheese to sauce and season to taste with nutmeg, salt, and pepper. Stir in egg yolks and set the sauce aside to keep warm.

3. Beat egg whites just until they hold stiff peaks. Remove sauce from the heat and stir a fourth of the egg whites into the sauce. Fold remaining whites into the sauce with a wide spatula. Immediately pour mixture into the baking dish and place it in the upper half of the oven.

4. Reduce heat to 350° F and bake 25 to 30 minutes, or until the soufflé is puffy and lightly browned and a skewer or knife inserted into the center comes out moist but clean. Serve immediately.

Serves 2 as a main course or 4 as a first course.

Variation A number of different cheeses can be used in place of the blue cheese. Mild goat cheeses like the French Montrachet or the newer California goat cheeses are good, especially with a white wine. Other choices for soufflés include the Swiss and Cheddar types and Brie or Camembert with the rind removed.

VINAIGRETTE WITH GOAT CHEESE

The tang of goat cheese lets you use less acid in the vinaigrette, making this a salad dressing that goes better than most with wine.

- 1 tablespoon lemon juice or 2 teaspoons mild vinegar Pinch salt Large pinch pepper
- ¼ cup olive oil
- 2 ounces mild, crumbly goat cheese

1. In a large salad bowl, combine lemon juice, salt, and pepper. Stir to dissolve the salt.

2. Add oil in a thin stream, stirring constantly to blend the dressing. Taste and adjust the proportions to your taste.

3. Crumble cheese into bowl. With your fingertips or the back of the fork, mash some of the cheese to a paste and combine it thoroughly with the dressing. The bowl is now ready to receive the greens.

Makes about ⅓ cup (3 to 4 servings).

Blue Cheese Vinaigrette Substitute Roquefort, aged Gorgonzola, Maytag or other domestic blue cheese, or Danish blue cheese for the goat cheese in the above dressing.

WINE AND DESSERT

Sweet table wines or fortified wines are sometimes referred to as "dessert wines." Does this mean that they can or should be served alongside dessert? Maybe. However, the best wine to serve with a given dessert may not be a "dessert wine."

Some of the wines that are mentioned as accompaniments to dessert are late-harvest Riesling, Gewürztraminer, or Sauvignon Blanc; sweet table wines like Muscat and some Rieslings, Gewürztraminers, and Chenin Blancs; sparkling wines, both sweet and dry; and the sweeter sherries, ports, and fortified Muscat wines. In many cases, a glass of one of these wines can serve as dessert in itself, or perhaps combined with a little cheese and a piece of fruit. With care, most of them can be matched to a dessert, but they are hardly all-purpose "dessert wines."

The key to matching wines with desserts is balance, especially the balance of sweetness and other flavors. As a rule, very sweet desserts are difficult to match with wines, and very sweet wines do not necessarily go well with desserts. Slightly sweet desserts and slightly sweet wines offer the best combinations.

For example, combining ice cream with a sweet wine results in too much sweetness, but a dry wine tastes sour next to something so sweet. Even a wine with just the right amount of sweetness is likely to taste thin next to the creamy richness of the dessert. The one wine that might go well with ice cream would be a rich "medium-dry" sherry.

Simple cakes and sweet biscuits are the best desserts to accompany sweet wines. A delicate sponge cake, perhaps with a fresh fruit filling but without any sweet icing, can go with an intensely sweet (8 to 10 percent residual sugar) late-harvest Riesling. But if you increase the sweetness of the dessert, be sure to decrease the sweetness of the wine to maintain a balance. Add a sweetened icing of whipped cream and white chocolate to the same cake and a wine of about 2 percent residual sugar provides a perfect counterpoint.

Desserts that emphasize fresh fruit flavors also marry well with light, slightly sweet wines. Pears poached in a light syrup, for example, can be served with a Muscat Blanc or Gewürztraminer. In fact, the same wine can be used to poach the fruit. Another simple but delicious combination is assorted fruits marinated in sweet wine (see page 95).

Chocolate and wine may seem an unusual combination, but there are some wines that go well with chocolate desserts. If the dessert is not too sweet, a medium sherry or tawny port might be a good match. Quady Winery suggests chocolate mousse with its "Essencia," a fortified Orange Muscat. But if your taste runs to dense, dark, bittersweet chocolate cakes, skip the sweet wines and try a glass of a big Cabernet Sauvignon. The combination may surprise you! Strong, aromatic, slightly bitter and astringent, the wine, like a cup of dark-roast coffee, offers a satisfying balance to the equally intense flavor and buttery richness of the chocolate.

WINE SORBET

This delicate frozen dessert can be made from just about any table wine except a really tannic red. You can also use a sweet wine, but reduce the sugar in the syrup by a tablespoon. Riesling or White Zinfandel would be good wines to start with, but feel free to experiment with various whites, rosés, and reds.

Alcohol affects the freezing process, so don't omit the step of boiling half the wine with the syrup; this removes some, but not all, of the alcohol, giving the sorbet just the right texture and flavor. The sorbet does not keep well, as it tends to separate in the freezer.

    1 cup water
    ½ cup sugar
    1 cup dry or slightly sweet table wine

1. *One day ahead:* Combine water, sugar, and half the wine in a saucepan. Stir to dissolve sugar; bring to a boil. Reduce heat and simmer 3 minutes. Allow syrup to cool.

2. Add remaining wine to syrup. Pour into a shallow container and freeze overnight.

3. *Two to four hours ahead:* Remove frozen mixture from freezer. Transfer to a food processor and process until smooth, about 20 to 30 seconds. Return mixture to freezer container or individual serving glasses and return to the freezer to set.

4. Remove sorbet from the freezer 5 to 10 minutes before serving.

Serves 8.

APRICOT-ORANGE MUSCAT SPONGE CAKE

This cake is a perfect example of how a not-too-sweet dessert can complement a sweet wine. The dried apricot filling, tart and full of flavor, finds an echo in the apricot aromas of the wine. A late-harvest Riesling would also work nicely. Serve with a glass of the same wine.

    1½ cups dried apricots
    1 cup Quady Orange Muscat "Essencia"
    4 eggs
    ⅔ cup sugar
    ½ teaspoon vanilla extract
    ¾ cup sifted cake flour
    3 tablespoons unsalted butter, melted and kept barely warm
    1½ cups whipping cream
    ½ cup sliced almonds

1. Place apricots in a small bowl, add wine, and soak until apricots are soft, 2 hours or more, turning apricots occasionally to marinate them evenly.

2. Preheat oven to 350° F. Butter and lightly flour a 9- by 2-inch round cake pan; line the bottom with a piece of waxed paper.

3. Place eggs and sugar in a 4-quart stainless steel mixing bowl over a pot of boiling water and whisk until mixture is warm to the touch. Immediately remove from heat, add vanilla, and beat (with whisk or electric mixer) until batter will hold a crease (a fingertip or spatula drawn through top of batter leaves a depression that fills in very slowly). Sift flour over batter, folding it in with a rubber spatula as lightly and quickly as possible. Stir ½ cup of batter into butter, then fold butter mixture quickly and gently into remaining batter.

4. Pour batter into prepared pan and bake until top of cake springs back when lightly touched, 25 to 30 minutes. Cool in pan 5 minutes, then turn out onto rack to finish cooling. If you wish, while cake is cooling, you can trim off and discard browned top and bottom.

5. Drain apricots, reserving wine. With a food processor or by hand, chop apricots finely adding a little wine if necessary for more thorough chopping.

6. Whip cream to the soft-peak stage. Set aside 2 tablespoons of chopped apricots for decoration. Combine remaining apricots with 1 cup of the whipped cream.

7. *To assemble cake:* With a long, serrated knife, split the cake horizontally into 2 equal layers. Remove the top layer. Brush bottom layer lightly with wine until it is evenly moistened but not soggy. Spread the apricot-cream mixture evenly over the bottom layer, spreading it just to the edge of the cake. Brush cut side of top layer of cake with remaining wine, adding a little more wine if necessary. Place top layer on top of cake. Spread top and sides of cake evenly with remaining whipped cream. Press a thin layer of sliced almonds against sides of cake. Decorate top with 10 or 12 evenly spaced dots of chopped apricots, *or* combine apricots with a little whipped cream, place mixture in a pastry bag with a star tip, and decorate top with 10 or 12 rosettes. Refrigerate until cream is firm, at least 1 hour.

Serves 10 to 12.

Light, refreshing Wine Sorbet can be made from just about any table wine except perhaps a very tannic young red. Serve it with cookies as a dessert, or try it as an interlude between courses of a fancy meal.

MATCHING THE MENU TO THE WINES

For everyday meals and casual entertaining, you will probably want to serve just one wine, chosen to go with the main dish. In most of the wine-drinking world, the same wine is served with every dish. But when serving a meal of several courses, you may want to serve different wines with different courses. The general rule on the sequence of wines is to progress from lighter to heavier, younger to older, dry to sweet, and lesser wines to greater. Exceptions can be made, of course, when the sequence of dishes in the menu suggests another order.

A traditional menu of several courses and several wines might read like the following:

*Mushroom Caps With
Chicken Liver Stuffing
(page 61)*

*Christian Brothers
Dry Sherry*

Shellfish Bisque (page 65)

*Jekel Monterey
Johannisberg Riesling*

*Steak Marchand de Vin
(page 73)
Broiled Tomatoes
Shoestring Potatoes
Mixed Greens Vinaigrette*

*Ridge Monte Bello
Cabernet Sauvignon*

Raspberry Tart

Coffee and Liqueurs

A more elaborate menu might start with Champagne and caviar, then proceed to dry sherry with a consommé, Sauvignon Blanc with a poached fish dish, two Cabernets of different vintages with roast or grilled lamb and the cheese course, and a late-harvest Riesling with a fruit dessert.

Of course, not all menus with several wines need be this complicated. On the following pages are a variety of menus combining foods and wines.

menu

A SOUTHEAST ASIAN MENU

*Spicy Meatballs With
Peanut Sauce (page 62)*

*Chicken With Red Peppers
and Basil*

Sour Catfish Soup

*Vegetable Curry With
Coconut Milk*

Steamed Rice

*Pedroncelli Johannisberg
Riesling
or
Arbor Crest White Riesling*

Recent immigrants from Southeast Asia have brought a whole new world of exotic flavors to American markets. Coconut milk, tamarind (the sour-tasting seedpods of a tropical tree), lemongrass, fermented shrimp paste, and bottled fish sauce are among the foods of this region that are starting to appear in more and more American cities. If stores in your area stock these foods, why not add a few Southeast Asian dishes to your repertoire of international foods?

Authentic Thai, Indonesian, or Malaysian foods may be too hot for many Americans. The following recipes are somewhat toned-down versions, designed to go better with wine. Even so, this is not the place for "serious" white wines; serve a light, fruity wine, perhaps slightly sweet. Chenin Blanc, Riesling, Gewürztraminer, or extra-dry sparkling wine would go nicely with these exuberantly flavored dishes.

Of course, if you like your food very hot, feel free to add more hot pepper, either in the form of prepared chile condiments (sambals) or by using fresh or dried chiles as part of the sauces themselves.

CHICKEN WITH RED PEPPERS AND BASIL

1 large chicken breast, boned and cut into bite-sized pieces
¼ cup Thai, Vietnamese, or Philippine fish sauce (nuoc mam; see Note) or soy sauce
1 large red bell pepper or 2 to 4 fresh red chiles
½ cup coconut milk (see Note)
2 tablespoons oil
2 tablespoons minced fresh ginger
2 tablespoons minced garlic
1 or 2 green onions (white and green parts), thinly sliced
½ cup (loosely packed) fresh basil leaves
Salt to taste

1. In a small bowl combine chicken pieces and fish sauce and set aside.

2. Remove core, seeds, and veins from red pepper; cut into large dice.

3. Drain chicken well, straining liquid into coconut milk. Heat oil in a wok or large skillet over medium-high heat. Add ginger, garlic, and green onion; stir and cook until fragrant, about 30 seconds. Add pepper, stir and cook another 30 seconds. Add chicken, stir and cook until chicken begins to stiffen and turn white, about 1 minute.

4. Add coconut milk mixture and basil. Bring to a boil, reduce heat, and simmer until chicken is done and sauce thickens slightly. Taste for seasoning and add salt or fish sauce to taste.

5. Transfer to a serving dish and serve over bowls of rice.

Makes 4 servings as part of a multicourse meal, or 2 main-course servings.

Note Available in Asian groceries.

SOUR CATFISH SOUP

1 ounce tamarind pulp (see Note)
4 cups hot water
1 tablespoon oil
2 tablespoons minced fresh ginger
2 green onions, thinly sliced
1 stalk lemongrass, thinly sliced
Pinch hot pepper flakes
2 tablespoons fish sauce
Lemon juice to taste
½ pound catfish fillets
Cucumber slices, for garnish

1. Soak tamarind pulp in the hot water until it is soft.

2. Heat oil in a medium saucepan over medium heat. Add ginger, green onions, lemongrass, and hot pepper flakes and cook just until fragrant, about 30 seconds.

3. Strain tamarind water through a fine-mesh strainer into the same saucepan. With a wooden spoon, push pulp through strainer into the saucepan, straining out and discarding seeds and fibers. Add fish sauce to pan. Simmer 5 minutes and taste for seasoning—it should be tart and slightly hot. Adjust seasonings if necessary. (May be prepared to this point up to an hour ahead.)

4. Have soup at a simmer. Add catfish slices and cook just until opaque white. Serve immediately, garnished with cucumber slices.

Serves 4.

Note Whole tamarind pods are available in Asian and Latin American markets, but an easier form to use is the blocks of prepared tamarind pulp sold in Asian shops. A few shops carry a liquid tamarind extract, which is more expensive but requires no straining.

VEGETABLE CURRY WITH COCONUT MILK

2 tablespoons oil
1 large onion, sliced
3 cloves garlic, minced
2 tablespoons minced fresh ginger
½ teaspoon ground turmeric
½ teaspoon ground cumin
¼ teaspoon cardamom seed, crushed
Pinch ground cloves
⅛ teaspoon cayenne pepper
2½ cups coconut milk
¼ cup fish sauce
3 cups assorted vegetables in bite-sized pieces (cauliflower and broccoli florets, new potatoes, green beans, zucchini, tomatoes, carrots, celery, Chinese cabbage, spinach, chard)
Salt and freshly ground pepper to taste

1. Heat oil in a wok or saucepan over medium heat. Sauté onion, garlic, and ginger until fragrant but not browned, about 1 minute. Stir in turmeric, cumin, cardamom, cloves, and cayenne and cook 5 minutes. Add coconut milk and fish sauce; bring to a boil.

2. Reduce heat to a simmer. Add vegetables, beginning with firmest types and cooking them until nearly tender before adding softer vegetables. Simmer until slightly thickened. Taste for seasoning and adjust if necessary. Serve over rice.

Serves 4.

ALL–PINOT NOIR MENU

*Grilled Chicken Salad With
Almonds and Cucumbers*

*Sebastiani
Pinot Noir Blanc*

*Red-Wine Fish Stew
(page 65)*

*Focaccia (Italian-style
olive oil bread)*

Adelsheim Pinot Noir

Fruit and Cheese

---

*This is a delightful
menu for those in-
between seasons
when warm days
quickly give way to
chilly evenings. Fresh
and fruity but dry,
with a deeper flavor
than most white
wines, the Pinot Noir
blanc is an
especially good
match with cold
chicken and
mustard. Other good
choices would be a
Sanford or Edna
Valley Pinot Noir Vin
Gris, or a dry white
Zinfandel. The fish
stew demands a*

*wine with good acid-
ity, but fairly mild
flavor; Oregon Pinot
Noir fits the bill ex-
actly, but some of the
lighter Pinots from
California's Car-
neros region, such as
Buena Vista or
Saintsbury, would
also go well.*

GRILLED CHICKEN SALAD WITH ALMONDS AND CUCUMBERS

- ¼ cup blanched slivered almonds
- 1 large chicken breast (1 lb), grilled and cooled
- 1 tablespoon Dijon mustard
- 1 tablespoon lemon juice
- ¼ cup olive oil
  Pinch salt
  Pepper to taste
- 1 large cucumber, peeled, halved, seeded, and sliced
  Outer leaves of butter lettuce or red-leaf lettuce

1. Toast almonds in a small, dry skillet, shaking or stirring constantly so they brown evenly. Set aside.

2. Shred chicken meat by hand or with a knife. Slice skin into thin strips if desired, or discard it.

3. In a medium bowl, combine mustard, lemon juice, oil, salt, and pepper. Blend thoroughly, taste, and adjust the seasonings as necessary. Toss the chicken, almonds, and cucumbers in the dressing. Serve the salad on large lettuce leaves.

Serves 4.

A MEXICAN-INSPIRED MENU

*Enchiladas Verdes de
Mariscos*

*Christian Brothers Napa
Fumé Blanc*

Gallina en Mole (page 67)

*Monterey Peninsula
Vineyard "Doctor's
Reserve" Merlot
or
Monticello Albemarle
County Merlot*

*Avocado, Jicama, and
Grapefruit Salad*

---

*Although Mexican
food is usually
associated with beer,
many dishes, such as
Seviche, can be
served with wine,
especially if you tone
down the chiles.
These seafood
enchiladas are
perfectly matched
with an assertive
Sauvignon Blanc.
The same wine can
carry over to the
Gallina en Mole, or
you might prefer a
full-flavored red.*

ENCHILADAS VERDES DE MARISCOS
Seafood enchiladas with green sauce

2 tablespoons oil
2 tablespoons minced garlic
3 green onions, minced
1 or 2 fresh or canned green (Anaheim) chiles, finely chopped
1 can (12 oz) tomatillos (Mexican green tomatoes), puréed in a blender or food processor
¼ cup chopped cilantro
2 cups cooked shellfish (shrimp, crabmeat, scallops, or a combination)
8 corn tortillas
½ cup sour cream
½ cup grated jack or Swiss cheese

1. Preheat oven to 400° F. Heat oil in a large skillet over moderate heat. Add garlic, green onions, and chiles and cook until vegetables are soft but not browned. Stir in the tomatillo purée and cook mixture 10 minutes over low heat, adding a little water if the sauce starts to dry out. Add salt to taste.

2. Combine cilantro and shellfish in a bowl; stir in a small amount of the sauce. Moisten bottom of a shallow 8-by 13-inch baking dish with about ¼ cup of the sauce.

3. Dip a tortilla into the simmering sauce until soft and pliable, about 30 seconds; transfer to prepared baking dish. Place ¼ cup of the seafood across the center of tortilla and roll it into a cylinder. Repeat with remaining tortillas, fitting them snugly side by side. Pour remaining sauce over enchiladas, top each one with a spoonful of sour cream, and sprinkle cheese over the top. Bake 10 minutes and serve with the sauce from the baking pan.

Makes 8 enchiladas (4 main-course or 8 first-course servings).

AVOCADO, JICAMA, AND GRAPEFRUIT SALAD

1 large or 2 small avocados
2 medium ruby grapefruit
½ pound jicama
2 tablespoons olive oil
Salt and freshly ground pepper to taste

1. Peel avocado and cut into wedges. Cut away peel of grapefruit and cut the fruit into sections, reserving juice. Peel a section of jicama and slice it into thin wedges.

2. Alternate pieces of avocado, grapefruit, and jicama in a circle on a round serving plate or on individual plates. Combine reserved grapefruit juice, olive oil, and salt and pepper to taste. Drizzle dressing over salad.

Serves 4.

The distinctive "grassy" flavor and aroma of Sauvignon Blanc are a good match for the exuberant flavors of green chile, cilantro, and tomatillo in Enchiladas Verdes de Mariscos.

ALL-CHARDONNAY
MENU

*Cucumber Slices With
Smoked Trout or Albacore*

*Fettucine With White
Truffles*

*Steamed Salmon With
Tarragon (page 66)*

Selected Chardonnays

Warm Apple Tart

*Here is a menu
designed for a
Chardonnay tasting.
Rather than serve a
different wine with
each course, you may
want to pour all the
wines at once, and
let each diner choose.
For an interesting
comparison, try
Chardonnays made
in different styles:
say, a big, rich wine
such as Edna Valley
or Chateau St. Jean
next to a lighter,
fruitier one such as
Beaulieu or a
middle-of-the-road*

*wine like Robert
Mondavi or the Clos
du Bois Flintwood.
As with the following
menu, salmon is the
centerpiece of this
meal, but in this case
it is the milder-
flavored spring
salmon.*

FETTUCINE WITH WHITE
TRUFFLES

    2 tablespoons butter
    1 tablespoon minced shallot
    1 cup whipping cream
       A white truffle
    2 ounces Italian Fontina cheese
       Salt and freshly ground
       pepper to taste
    1 pound fettucine, preferably
       fresh, cooked in lightly
       salted water

1. Boil water for the pasta. The sauce
will take about 5 minutes to make, so
time the pasta accordingly.

2. Melt butter in a large skillet over
medium heat. Add shallots and cook
until soft and translucent. Pour in
cream, turn the heat to high, and
reduce cream by half.

3. While sauce is reducing, use a
vegetable peeler to shave off enough
tiny slices of truffle to make about a
tablespoon.

4. When cream begins to thicken,
add cheese and stir until it is melted.
Season sauce to taste, turn down heat,
and keep it at a simmer until the
noodles are ready.

5. Drain noodles thoroughly. Add
truffle shavings to sauce, then immediately toss the noodles in the sauce.
Serve immediately on warm plates
with a little freshly ground pepper.

*Serves 3 to 4 as a main dish, 6 as a
first course.*

ALL-CABERNET MENU

*Blue Cheese Soufflé
(page 79)*

*Glen Ellen "Proprietor's
Reserve" Cabernet
Sauvignon
or
Beaulieu "Beautour"
Cabernet Sauvignon*

*Charcoal-Grilled Salmon
Steaks With Grilled
Vegetables*

*Jordan Cabernet
Sauvignon
or
Robert Mondavi
Cabernet Sauvignon*

*Bittersweet Chocolate
Hazelnut Cake*

*This menu is
especially good late
in the summer, when
the ocean-caught
salmon are at their
richest and most
flavorful. Start with
a Cabernet made in
a lighter style, then
serve a well-aged
bottle of classic
Cabernet from
California's Napa or
Sonoma valleys with
the salmon and
dessert.*

CHARCOAL-GRILLED SALMON STEAKS WITH GRILLED VEGETABLES

> 4 salmon steaks, 6 to 8
> ounces each
> Salt and freshly ground
> black pepper
> Olive or vegetable oil
> 2 small zucchini and 2 small
> yellow crookneck squash,
> split lengthwise
> 8 green onions, trimmed
> 2 teaspoons dried thyme

1. Prepare a hot charcoal fire and preheat the grill. Remove salmon from the refrigerator at least 20 minutes before cooking. Season steaks lightly with salt and pepper and rub them with a little oil.

2. Season squashes with salt and pepper and rub them with a little oil.

Grill squashes and green onions until they begin to soften, then move them to the edge of the fire.

3. Toss a teaspoon or so of thyme leaves onto the coals and place the salmon steaks over the hottest part of the fire. Grill the steaks, turning only once, until a skewer easily penetrates the thickest part of the meat, about 6 to 10 minutes total cooking time, depending on thickness. Toss the remaining thyme into the fire when turning the steaks. Serve each steak with a slice of each squash and a couple of scallions.

Serves 4.

A Note on Timing Start the charcoal fire about the time you put the soufflé in the oven. If you are eating outdoors by the fire, the fish and vegetables can cook while you are eating the soufflé.

This All-Cabernet Menu presents some combinations that may surprise your guests—Cabernet with salmon and Cabernet with chocolate. The meal starts with an individual blue-cheese soufflé, accompanied by a lighter version of the wine. The grilled salmon and vegetables are matched to a fuller-bodied Cabernet, which also complements the bittersweet chocolate cake.

Chinese dishes, like this one of steamed vegetables with thin strips of Smithfield ham, can be served with a wide variety of American wines.

menu

A CHINESE MENU

*Stir-Fried Shrimp With
Ginger and Garlic*

*Firestone Santa Ynez
Valley Gewürztraminer
or
Charles Krug
Chenin Blanc*

*Red-Cooked Chicken
(page 96)*

*Steamed Vegetables With
Smithfield Ham*

Steamed Rice

*Buena Vista Sonoma
Valley Carneros Pinot Noir
or
Eyrie Vineyard Yamhill
County Pinot Noir*

*Chinese cuisine is
based on a balance
of the Five Flavors—
sweet, sour, salty,
bitter, and hot. These
flavors are usually
balanced within the
meal and the food
does not "need"
wine to complete the
harmony of flavors.
Still, those of us who
enjoy wine are
always looking for
new food and wine
combinations, and
Chinese food offers a
whole new range of
opportunities.*

*Gewürztraminer is
often recommended
with dishes that con-
tain ginger, garlic,
and pepper, like the
shrimp dish in the
following menu. Oth-
er white wines, espe-
cially Chenin Blancs,
are popular because
they refresh without
adding an assertive
flavor of their own.
But anyone who
thinks only white
wines go with Chi-
nese meals should
try a fine Pinot Noir
with "red-cooked"
duck or chicken
(simmered in a soy
sauce–based broth
with sweet spices),
a truly great East-
West combination.*

STEAMED VEGETABLES WITH SMITHFIELD HAM

4 cups assorted fresh vegetables,
  cut into bite-sized pieces:
  Chinese cabbage (bok choy,
  pak choy); red, green, or
  yellow bell peppers; broccoli
  or Chinese broccoli; carrots;
  snow peas
2 ounces Smithfield ham
  or prosciutto
1 tablespoon soy sauce
1 tablespoon Chinese or
  Japanese sesame oil

1. Steam vegetables until just tender.
Meanwhile, slice ham 1/16 inch thick;
stack slices of ham and slice again
crosswise into thin strips. Combine
soy sauce and sesame oil.

2. Transfer steamed vegetables to a
serving platter. Scatter ham over vegetables. Drizzle soy sauce mixture
over and serve immediately.

Serves 4 to 6 as a side dish.

STIR-FRIED SHRIMP WITH GINGER AND GARLIC

¼ cup dry white wine
2 tablespoons soy sauce
1 teaspoon vinegar
  Pinch sugar
1 pound shrimp or prawns,
  peeled and deveined
1 tablespoon minced
  fresh ginger
1 tablespoon minced garlic
2 tablespoons minced
  green onion
3 tablespoons peanut or other
  vegetable oil

1. Combine wine, soy sauce, vinegar,
and sugar in a bowl large enough to
marinate the shrimp. Stir to dissolve
the sugar. Toss shrimp in marinade
and set aside for 20 minutes or so.

2. Combine ginger, garlic, and green
onion in another bowl and set aside.

3. Have all the ingredients and tools
at hand and the rest of the dinner
ready to serve. Remove shrimp from
marinade and drain well, reserving
marinade. Heat a wok or large skillet
over medium-high heat. When pan is
hot, add oil in a thin stream around
pan and let it run into center. Add
ginger-garlic-green onion mixture to
pan, adjust heat so mixture sizzles but
does not burn, and stir-fry until very
fragrant, about 30 seconds. Add
drained shrimp and stir-fry until they
begin to stiffen, about 30 seconds.
Pour in marinade; stir and cook until
liquid is nearly all evaporated. If
shrimp need a little more cooking,
add a few tablespoons of water and
cook until it has evaporated. Sauce
should cling to shrimp, leaving almost none in pan. Transfer shrimp to
a serving dish and serve immediately.

*Serves 4 to 6 as part of a multi-
course meal.*

Good cooking begins with the best ingredients. Good, inexpensive wine from a quality winery is an important item for your pantry.

Cooking With Wine

Not only is wine an ideal
beverage to serve with
foods, it can also be an
important ingredient in cooking.
Throughout the winemaking regions of the
world are found classic dishes that
rely on the flavor of a particular wine
used in their preparation. Many of
these famous recipes, such as
beef bourgignon, veal Marsala, and
Madeira sauce, actually take their names
from the wine. In this chapter cooking
with wine is discussed by
technique, with original recipes
demonstrating each
technique.

A WINE-BASED CUISINE

Here in America, where our wine industry is still fairly young, we have not had as much time as the Europeans have had to develop a wine-based national cuisine. However, American cooking is constantly becoming more international in its scope, and more and more cooks are discovering the many uses of wine in the kitchen.

Understanding the basics of cooking with wine can add a whole range of flavors to your kitchen repertoire. Wine has three main uses in the kitchen: as a marinade ingredient, as a cooking liquid, and as a flavoring ingredient in the finished dish. Marinating food (especially meat and poultry) in wine adds flavor and tenderness. Wine can also be used as the cooking medium: poaching and braising in wine are two particularly useful techniques. And an ounce or two of the right wine can be just the thing to complete a sauce, whether for a simple sautéed dish or a roast.

All of these techniques are illustrated in the recipes in this chapter. Once you have mastered these, you will likely find many more uses for wine in your cooking. Wine can be used in place of part or all of the cooking or marinating liquid in countless recipes, as long as you observe the following rules:

☐ Boiling down wine concentrates its flavors, including acidity and sweetness. Be careful not to use too much or the finished dish may be too sweet, too sour, or too "winy."

☐ Whether making a quick deglazing sauce or a long-simmered dish, allow enough cooking time after adding the wine that the alcohol will evaporate. Boiling a sauce rapidly in a shallow pan will cook off the alcohol in a minute or two, but slow simmering in a deeper pan may take 15 minutes or more to achieve the same effect. Taste the sauce before serving to be sure. Avoid adding wine to a sauce just before serving, or the dish may taste unpleasantly alcoholic.

☐ Remember that wine does not belong in every dish. More than one wine-based sauce in a single meal can be monotonous, or, if different wines are used, the effect can be confusing to the palate. Use wine in cooking only when it has something to contribute to the dish.

WINES FOR THE KITCHEN

Choosing cooking wines is not quite as complicated as choosing the ideal wine to serve with a given food, but it must still be done with care. The basic rule is to use a good wine. Cooking a wine usually concentrates its flavor, so the wine itself should be a good-tasting one. In fact, good and bad wines have only two things in common: water and alcohol. Both of these evaporate in cooking, leaving behind just the ingredients that distinguish one wine from another.

Dry table wines are the most versatile category of cooking wines. With their wide range of flavors—from light, fruity whites to full-bodied, complex reds—table wines can provide either a subtle touch of flavor or a dominant theme. Sweeter table wines have more limited uses; cooking down a sauce containing a sweet wine would concentrate the sweetness too much for many dishes. For poached fruit or other desserts, however, a sweet wine may be ideal.

Fortified wines are another important category of cooking wines. The more concentrated flavors of sherry and port wines allow the cook to get more taste per ounce of wine.

Vermouth and other flavored wines add the additional taste of herbs and other aromatics. Both flavored and fortified wines should be used with care or they can give too strong a flavor to the food.

The wines referred to here are the same kinds of wines you might drink, not the so-called cooking wines sold in some stores. The latter are a peculiarly American invention— wines that are no longer considered alcoholic beverages, having been salted to the point that they are unfit to drink. The only advantage of these concoctions is that they can be sold in stores that do not have liquor or wine licenses and in "dry" states or localities. The wines are rarely very good in the first place, so you are much better off using a "real" wine of the same type instead.

Any wine good enough to cook with should be good enough to drink. A half-empty bottle of wine that has been sitting in the kitchen cabinet for a month is not likely to taste very good, and may in fact have turned to vinegar. You wouldn't want to use moldy cheese or spoiled cream in a recipe, so why take a chance with spoiled wine?

As a rule, the best cooking wine for a dish is the same type of wine you would serve with it. This doesn't mean that if you are serving a lamb roast with a fine old Cabernet you should marinate the lamb in another bottle of the same vintage. But a modestly priced, well-made younger Cabernet, preferably from the same general area, would be a better choice for the marinade than whatever other red wine you may happen to have around.

An assortment of fresh seasonal fruits marinated in sweet Muscat wine (see page 95) is the perfect finish to a summer meal.

Spicy Red-Wine Marinade (opposite page) gives a flavor boost to grilled Rock Cornish hens, shown here with grilled fennel, pecan-flavored rice, and a lighter-style Cabernet.

MARINATING WITH WINE

The right marinade can work wonders on a piece of meat or poultry. Even a brief time in a marinade can add flavor and moisture, and longer marinating can make tougher cuts of meat more tender. Wine is a perfect ingredient for both purposes. Besides adding a flavor of its own, the wine helps the food absorb the flavors of herbs, vegetables, or spices. The moderate acidity of wine also helps penetrate and tenderize meats.

Here are two wine marinades, each designed to give a deeper, more gamelike flavor to domestic meats and poultry.

PORK ROAST WITH WHITE-WINE MARINADE

Two days of marinating in a mixture of white wine, spices, and herbs gives roast pork a little of the flavor of wild boar.

> 1 teaspoon fennel seed
> 2 teaspoons coriander seed
> 1 teaspoon black peppercorns
> 1 teaspoon salt
> ¼ teaspoon ground ginger
> 1 pork loin roast, about 3½ pounds with bones
> 1 cup Gewürztraminer or Sauvignon Blanc
> 1 large sprig fresh sage or ½ teaspoon dried
> 1 large sprig fresh thyme or ½ teaspoon dried
> 1 bay leaf
> 8 small new potatoes, whole

1. *Two days ahead:* Coarsely grind the fennel, coriander, and pepper in a mortar or spice grinder. Combine ground spices with salt and ginger. Rub this mixture all over the pork roast. Put roast in a stainless steel, ceramic, or glass bowl, pour in wine, and crumble herbs into the bowl. Marinate the roast in the refrigerator, turning it several times a day to marinate it evenly.

2. *On cooking day:* Remove roast from the refrigerator at least an hour before cooking. Preheat oven to 450° F. Drain roast thoroughly and discard the marinade.

3. Pat roast dry with paper towels and place it fat side up on a rack in a roasting pan. Put roast in hot oven, reduce the heat to 325° F, and roast to an internal temperature of 170° F (25 to 30 minutes per pound). Add potatoes to the roasting pan for the last 30 minutes to roast in the drippings.

4. Let the roast rest about 15 minutes before carving into ½-inch slices. Serve with the roast potatoes and a full-flavored dry white wine or a lighter red wine.

Serves 4.

SPICY RED-WINE MARINADE

This recipe, similar to the pork marinade but based on a red wine, is especially good for roasted, broiled, or grilled poultry. For a sweeter taste, use ruby port instead of a dry wine.

> ½ teaspoon each *whole coriander, fennel, black pepper, and juniper berries*
> ¾ cup *dry red wine*
> 2 tablespoons *red wine vinegar*
> *Half an onion, sliced*
> 2 or 3 cloves *garlic, minced*
> 1 tablespoon *minced fresh ginger or ½ teaspoon ground ginger*

1. Grind the coriander, fennel, pepper, and juniper berries together in a spice grinder or mortar.

2. Combine the ground spices, wine, vinegar, onion, garlic, and ginger in a glass, ceramic, or stainless steel bowl large enough to hold the poultry.

3. Marinate whole or cut-up birds in the refrigerator, covered, overnight, or for up to 3 days. Turn the birds frequently to marinate them evenly.

4. Remove birds from the refrigerator 30 minutes before cooking. Drain thoroughly and discard marinade. Roast, grill, or broil (stuffed or unstuffed) according to any standard recipe.

Makes about 1 cup (enough for a whole fryer or duck or for 2 to 3 Rock Cornish hens).

FRESH FRUIT MARINATED IN WINE

Marinades for fruits are not intended to tenderize, as those for meats are, but rather serve to moisten the fruit and enhance their flavors. An assortment of seasonal fruits marinated in sweet Muscat wine makes a light, refreshing dessert. Of course, a glass of the same wine would taste fine along with it. Choose three or four of the following, depending on what is in season:

☐ Strawberries, hulled, split if large

☐ Cantaloupe, honeydew, or other *firm* melon, in cubes or balls

☐ Orange or tangerine sections, all white pith removed

☐ Peaches or nectarines, unpeeled, sliced

☐ Blueberries or huckleberries

☐ Red, green, or purple grapes, especially Muscat types

☐ Mango, peeled and cut into wedges

☐ Papaya, peeled and diced

☐ Pears, peeled, cored, and diced

☐ Fully ripe pineapple, in chunks

☐ Bananas, peeled and sliced

Actually, it is easier to list the fruits that do not work in this dish. Blackberries or boysenberries tend to disintegrate, and their juice stains the whole dish. Casaba melon can be too soft to hold together in the marinade, and watermelon adds a lot of liquid, diluting the flavor. Try to combine some tart fruits like oranges or pineapple with low-acid types like pears or bananas, but don't use too much tart fruit or the acidity will overpower the wine.

> 4 cups *assorted fresh fruit (see list above)*
> 1 cup *sweet Muscat Blanc, Muscat Canelli, or Malvasia Bianca*
> *Lemon juice to taste (omit if using citrus fruits)*
> *Mint leaves or borage blossoms*

1. Combine the cut-up fruit in a large bowl, pour in the wine and toss to moisten the fruit thoroughly with wine. Marinate in the refrigerator 1 to 4 hours.

2. Taste a piece of the sweetest fruit and a piece of the most tart. Add lemon juice if necessary. Serve with a garnish of fresh mint or borage blossoms.

Serves 4.

POACHING IN WINE

Cooking directly in wine is another way to add a wine flavor to foods. The simplest form is poaching— cooking the food in a simmering wine-based liquid.

Poaching in wine is ideal for delicate foods, especially fish. The poaching liquid may be a simple *court bouillon* of wine and water flavored with aromatics or a *fumet*, a wine-based fish stock. Remember, however, that poaching is not the same as boiling. To achieve the tender, moist texture of poached foods, you must cook them gently. For the best results the poaching liquid should barely simmer.

COURT BOUILLON

This aromatic liquid is the perfect base for delicate poached fish dishes or vegetables à la grecque. After poaching, the liquid can be strained and refrigerated or frozen for future use. Strong vegetables or fish will give their flavor to the court bouillon, so any reserved stock should only be used for the same type of foods.

> 3 cups *water*
> 1 cup *dry white wine*
> 3 sprigs *parsley*
> 1 *bay leaf*
> 1 small *onion, peeled and sliced, or 2 to 3 green onions, chopped*
> 1 teaspoon *cracked black peppercorns*
> ½ teaspoon *anise or fennel seed*

1. Combine all ingredients in a non-aluminum saucepan. Bring to a boil, reduce heat, and simmer 15 minutes.

2. Strain stock through a fine-mesh strainer and discard vegetables. The stock may be made up to 3 days ahead and refrigerated.

Makes 4 cups.

FUMET
White-wine fish stock

Leftover court bouillon can be used for all or part of the liquid in this recipe. Fumet freezes well. You can concentrate it by boiling it down so it can be frozen in smaller containers.

> 2 to 3 pounds heads, bones, and trimmings of lean white fish
> 1 large onion, peeled and diced
> 1 thin quarter-sized slice fresh ginger (optional)
>   Stems of 1 bunch parsley
> 1 bay leaf
> 1 celery leaf
> 1 teaspoon anise or fennel seed
> 1 teaspoon cracked peppercorns
>   Half a bottle dry white wine

1. Wash fish parts thoroughly to remove any trace of blood or organs. Remove the gills, if present, from the head. Split large heads with a cleaver or a heavy chef's knife.

2. Place fish parts, onion, ginger (if used), parsley stems, bay leaf, celery leaf, anise or fennel seed, and peppercorns in a large saucepan or stockpot. Add wine and enough water to cover (about 8 cups).

3. Bring to a boil, reduce heat, and simmer 30 to 45 minutes. Skim off any foam that rises to the surface. Strain finished stock through a fine-mesh strainer. If a stronger stock is desired, cook it further after straining. (Do not try to get a stronger stock by cooking the bones longer; this may cause bitter flavors to develop.) Use immediately, or refrigerate or freeze the fumet for future use.

Makes about 8 cups.

POACHED FISH STEAKS WITH FRESH HERBS AND CREAM

Poached fish may be served plain, but it is usually better with a sauce. Often the poaching liquid itself can be the basis for the sauce. This recipe can serve as a model for countless dishes; it can be made with different varieties of fish, for example, or with mushrooms, tomatoes, or shellfish added to the sauce. The variations are limited only by your imagination.

> 4 halibut, salmon, or turbot steaks, 1 inch thick
> ½ cup whipping cream
> 4 cups Court Bouillon (page 95) or Fumet (at left)
> 2 tablespoons chopped fresh herbs, such as chives, parsley, basil, or chervil
>   Salt and pepper to taste
>   Rind of half a lemon

1. Take fish and cream out of the refrigerator at least 15 minutes ahead of cooking to let them come to room temperature.

2. Choose a deep skillet just large enough to hold the fish steaks in one layer. Heat Court Bouillon or Fumet over moderate heat until it just reaches the simmering point. Slide fish steaks into the simmering stock. Adjust the heat so the stock simmers slowly, being careful not to let it boil.

3. Cook fish to the slightly underdone stage—about 7 minutes for salmon and 8 to 9 minutes for halibut or turbot. (To test for doneness, insert a thin skewer or toothpick into thickest part of fish. There should be some resistance in the center.) Transfer the almost-cooked steaks to a warm platter; cover loosely with foil to keep them warm.

4. Pour out half the liquid, reserving it for another use. Turn the heat to high and boil the stock until it is reduced by two thirds. Add cream and reduce the sauce until it is slightly thickened. Turn down the heat, stir in the herbs, and season to taste.

5. Return fish steaks to the skillet to reheat slightly in the sauce. Serve the steaks topped with the sauce and sprinkle a little lemon rind over the top of each.

Serves 4.

RED-COOKED CHICKEN

A whole chicken slowly simmered in a fragrant mixture of soy sauce, wine, fresh ginger, and spices is a classic northern Chinese dish. The term "red-cooked" refers to the lovely red-brown color the soy sauce gives to the skin. The simmering liquid or "master sauce" can be used over and over, and gets better each time. Chicken wings or other parts can be cooked in the sauce and served as an appetizer or picnic dish. Served with a Pinot Noir or Gamay Beaujolais, this dish fits equally well in either a Chinese or a Western menu.

> 1 whole chicken
> 2 cups water
> 2 cups soy sauce
> ½ cup white wine
> 2 tablespoons sugar (less if using a sweet wine)
> 5 thin slices fresh ginger
> 2 green onions, sliced
> 1½ whole pods star anise or 1 teaspoon Chinese five-spice powder (available in Chinese groceries)
>   Half a cinnamon stick, crumbled, or ½ teaspoon ground cinnamon
> 1 teaspoon sesame oil (optional)

1. Remove any excess fat from the cavity and neck end of the chicken. Clean the chicken thoroughly inside and out, and be sure to remove the kidneys, the soft red tissues tucked in against the backbone near the tail end. Rinse the bird well inside and out and pat dry with paper towels. Remove the wing tips if you like; otherwise tuck them behind the back.

2. Choose a covered casserole or saucepan that will just hold the chicken. Combine the water, soy sauce, wine, sugar, ginger, green onions, star anise, and cinnamon in the pan and bring to a boil, stirring to dissolve the sugar.

3. Slowly lower the chicken into the pan, breast side down. As the liquid returns to the boil, baste the exposed part of the chicken with the liquid to start coloring the skin. Reduce the heat to a simmer, cover, and cook 20 minutes, basting occasionally.

4. After 20 minutes, turn the chicken over, being careful not to tear the breast skin. (The easiest way to turn the bird is with two wooden spoons, one inside the cavity, one outside.) Cook another 30 minutes, basting every few minutes.

5. Turn off the heat and let the chicken rest in the sauce for at least 30 minutes and up to 2 hours. Baste frequently with the sauce to ensure a deep, even color, and keep the pan covered to keep in the heat.

6. Lift chicken out of pot and drain it thoroughly. Serve hot, lukewarm, or cold. For an attractive shine, rub or brush the skin with the optional sesame oil. Strain the sauce and refrigerate or freeze for future use.

Serves 3 to 4 as a main dish, 6 or more as part of a multicourse meal.

To reuse the sauce: Add half the amount of sugar and aromatics called for in the original recipe plus ½ cup soy sauce to the leftover sauce each time you reuse it. This keeps the balance of flavors about the same, and the fresh soy sauce gives the right color to the skin.

One of the simplest and finest ways to cook salmon (or almost any fish) is to poach it in a Court Bouillon made with dry white wine (see page 95). Reduce some of the poaching liquid and add cream for an instant sauce.

BRAISING IN WINE

Braising meats and poultry in wine—first browning the meat or poultry in oil or fat, then adding wine and cooking slowly in a covered pan—is a technique common to some of the world's most satisfying dishes. Not only does the wine help moisten and tenderize tougher cuts of meat, its distinctive flavor also enhances the sauce. The long, slow cooking and the typical final reduction of the sauce concentrate the flavors of the wine. This concentration, however, can be a mixed blessing. Red wines, especially, can dominate a sauce, so they should be used with caution.

Of course, there are times when the concentrated flavor of red wine is just what you want, as in the classic preparation of the Burgundian coq au vin. But with other dishes, even if you plan to serve a red wine, the more delicate flavor of a white may bring out the best flavors. The following recipes are examples of each: The first uses a white wine in a dish that can be served with some of the lighter reds, while the second calls for a full-bodied red, and should be served with the same sort of wine.

RABBIT SAUCE FOR PASTA

Serve this delicious Florentine specialty with a Pinot Noir or a Zinfandel made in a lighter style. If you prefer a white wine, try a Chardonnay or Sauvignon Blanc with plenty of body.

  1 cup dry white wine
  1 tablespoon wine vinegar
  1 small onion, sliced
  4 cloves garlic, lightly crushed
  1 cut-up rabbit, 2½ to 3 pounds
  2 tablespoons flour
  ½ teaspoon salt
  ¼ teaspoon pepper
  2 tablespoons olive oil
  ½ cup each diced carrot, celery, and onion

  1 bay leaf
  1 teaspoon chopped fresh sage or ½ teaspoon dried
  1 tablespoon tomato paste

1. Combine wine, vinegar, onion, and garlic in a large stainless steel, ceramic, or glass bowl. Toss rabbit parts, including the liver and kidneys, in the marinade. Marinate 6 hours or more, or overnight, turning the pieces several times to marinate them evenly. (If you are using a frozen rabbit, unwrap it a day ahead of time and let it thaw overnight in the refrigerator in the marinade.)

2. Remove rabbit pieces from marinade. Strain and reserve marinade; discard onion and garlic. Set aside liver and kidneys. Dry rabbit pieces well. Combine flour, salt, and pepper; toss rabbit pieces in seasoned flour.

3. In a heavy flameproof casserole with a tight-fitting lid over medium-high heat, heat oil. Brown rabbit pieces thoroughly, removing them from the pan once they are browned. Add diced carrot, celery, and onion and cook, stirring, until onion is translucent but not brown. Return rabbit pieces to pan and pour in reserved marinade. Add bay leaf and sage. Bring to a boil, reduce to a simmer, cover, and cook until meat is tender and nearly falling off the bones, about 1½ to 2 hours. While the rabbit is cooking, cut the liver and kidneys into ¼-inch cubes.

4. When the meat is tender, remove the pieces to a plate. Add the tomato paste and diced giblets to the pan. Turn up the heat, bring the sauce to a boil, and reduce it until it is thick enough to coat pasta. Meanwhile, as soon as the rabbit has become cool enough to handle, pull or cut the meat off the bones and cut it into ½-inch pieces. Return the meat to the sauce, taste for seasoning, and keep warm until ready to serve.

5. Serve the sauce over cooked fresh or dried fettucine or other wide egg noodles.

Serves 4 as a main course.

BEEF BRAISED IN RED WINE

This is not a dish for subtle wines; it works best with a big, full-flavored wine with ample acidity. A Petite Sirah or a Zinfandel with plenty of character will fill the bill nicely. Serve the same type of wine with it.

Although braised beef can be cooked on top of the stove, it is easier to maintain the slight simmer in a low oven. A slow cooker or other electric covered cooker also works well, but you will still need to do steps 1 through 3 on top of the stove.

  2½ pounds boneless chuck roast
  1 tablespoon oil or chicken or duck fat
  ⅓ pound shallots, peeled and left whole
    Half a bottle dry red wine
    Bouquet garni of parsley, bay leaf, thyme, and celery leaves (see Note)
  ½ teaspoon salt
  ½ teaspoon black pepper
  4 dried tomato halves, chopped or 8 dry-cured olives, pitted and chopped

1. Preheat oven to 225° F. Cut meat into large cubes (2 to 2½ inches), trimmed of excess fat and gristle. Dry the cubes of meat with a paper towel. (This allows them to brown more easily.)

2. In an ovenproof casserole over medium heat, heat oil. Brown cubes of meat a few at a time. (Don't try to brown too many at a time or they will stew rather than brown.) Transfer the cubes to a plate as they brown and add more as space allows.

3. When all the meat has been browned, brown shallots in the same fat. Pour out any fat remaining in the pan. Add wine, bring to a boil, and reduce heat to a simmer. Return meat cubes to the pan. Add bouquet garni, salt, pepper, and tomatoes or olives.

4. Cover pan and place it in the oven. Bake 3½ to 4 hours, adjusting the heat, if necessary, so the sauce barely simmers. The meat should be very tender and should absorb the flavor of the sauce.

5. Turn off oven. Remove cooked meat and shallots to a serving platter and return them to the oven to keep warm. Discard the bouquet garni and bring sauce to a boil on top of the stove. Reduce the sauce by a third. Taste and correct the seasoning.

6. Pour sauce over meat and serve with buttered noodles, steamed potatoes, or polenta.

Serves 6.

<u>Note</u> To make a bouquet garni, gather into a bundle 2 or 3 sprigs parsley, a sprig of fresh thyme, one of the pale yellow, leafy stalks in the center of a head of celery, and a bay leaf. Tie the bundle together with kitchen twine to make it easier to remove from the pot after cooking. An alternate way, especially useful with dried herbs, is to wrap them in cheesecloth, then tie the cloth into a loose bundle with twine.

Long, slow cooking gives deep, satisfying flavor to Beef Braised in Red Wine. Even after hours of cooking, the olives or dried tomatoes provide nuggets of intense flavor.

MAKING YOUR OWN WINE VINEGAR

Vinegar (from the French *vin aigre*, sour wine) is a natural fermentation product, like wine. It is produced by a type of bacteria that feeds on alcohol, converting it into acetic acid. Vinegar bacteria are present wherever fruits are grown, and are often transmitted by fruit flies. In fact, preventing spoilage by vinegar bacteria is a major concern in winemaking.

Making vinegar is a matter of encouraging such bacteria. All you need is a sound wine, a good-sized container, and a source of the vinegar bacteria. One possibility is a bottle of wine that is turning to vinegar on its own. Some unpasteurized wine vinegars contain enough bacteria to get your batch started. However, the most reliable source is a vinegar culture, which you can buy at some home winemaking supply stores. These cultures tend to be expensive, but once you have a good starter, you can keep it going indefinitely.

Use a good, dry table wine. Sweet wines should be avoided; the sugar interferes with the vinegar culture. Wines that have off flavors or aromas (other than a little vinegary aroma) will give the same flavors to the vinegar.

The simplest container for vinegar is a large bottle, preferably a jug holding 1.5 liters or more. Wash it thoroughly, then add 1 part each of vinegar culture and water and 2 parts dry wine, for a total volume about half of what the jug will hold, to allow good air circulation. Cover the jug with a loose plug of cotton or cheesecloth, or with a piece of nylon stocking stretched over the top and held with a rubber band. This cover keeps insects out but lets oxygen in. Set the jug in a warm place. The liquid should begin to smell and taste quite vinegary within a week or so, but it may take a couple of months to convert all the alcohol to vinegar. Once the vinegar culture is working, you can add diluted odds and ends of unfinished bottles of wine, 1 part water to 3 parts wine. However, take care not to fill the jug more than three-fourths full. If you need more space, start another jug, using some of your working vinegar as the culture.

When the vinegar is ready, decant it into bottles. It will eventually form a deposit in the bottle, like the sediment in an aged bottle of wine. This is harmless, but if you prefer a perfectly clear vinegar, filter it at bottling time through a coffee filter or cheesecloth. Leave enough vinegar in the jug to make the next batch of vinegar. Tightly sealed bottles of vinegar can be aged for several months or even years, which will give a smoother flavor.

If you really want to get serious about vinegar making, you might try making an oak-aged version. Winemaking supply stores carry small oak barrels and can provide instructions on how to make a vinegar barrel that will provide you with a continuous supply of delicious vinegar.

THE FINISHING TOUCH: WINE SAUCES

Experienced cooks know the importance of a good sauce. Frequently, the secret of a good sauce is the judicious use of wine. From simple sauces whipped up in a few minutes in a sauté pan to long-simmered brown sauces and wine-enriched gravies, wine sauces are valuable additions to any cook's repertoire.

Deglazing a roasting or sauté pan with wine is the first step in creating a delicious assortment of sauces. Whether you are working with a beef roast, pan-fried chicken, or sautéed fish filets, the basic procedure for deglazing is the same: remove the excess fat, add aromatics (herbs, onions, garlic), then add the wine and bring it to a boil, scraping the drippings loose from the pan. After the alcohol has boiled out of the wine, other liquids may be added. The three recipes that follow are examples of the range of sauces based on deglazing with wine. Another example of this technique is Sautéed Beef Steaks Marchand de Vin (see page 73).

Reducing

Most recipes for wine sauces call for "reducing," which simply means boiling down the sauce until its volume has been cut by about half. Reducing is an essential technique in many great sauces. When a sauce containing cream is sufficiently reduced, no other thickeners are needed. When a meat, poultry, or fish stock is reduced drastically, the gelatin in it can give the sauce enough body to make further thickening unnecessary. Reducing a wine-based sauce eliminates the alcohol while it concentrates the flavor of the wine.

Reduced sauces must be made with care. Reducing a wine sauce too far can make it too acidic, while at the same time boiling away most of the flavor. Salt, sugar, and other seasonings are also concentrated; for this reason, it is best to season a sauce only after it has been reduced.

CHICKEN BREASTS WITH SHERRY, CREAM, AND MUSHROOMS

If you are serving a first course before this dish, you can cook the chicken breasts first, then hold them in the oven for 15 minutes or so. The sauce will only take about five minutes to prepare, so you will be able to sit down and enjoy the first course before serving the entrée.

> 4 chicken breast halves, boned and skinned
> ¼ cup flour
> ½ teaspoon salt
> ½ teaspoon pepper
> 2 to 4 tablespoons butter
> 2 tablespoons vegetable oil
> ¼ pound mushrooms, sliced
> 1 tablespoon chopped garlic
> 1 green onion, chopped
> ¼ cup dry sherry
> ½ cup whipping cream

1. Preheat oven to 200° F. Trim all bits of fat and membrane from the chicken breasts. In a shallow bowl combine flour, salt, and pepper. Dredge breasts in the seasoned flour and shake off the excess. Have a warm, ovenproof plate ready.

2. In a large skillet over medium heat, heat butter and oil together. Add chicken breasts and cook just until the thickest part springs back when pressed, about 3 minutes per side. Remove to the warm plate, cover loosely with foil, and keep warm in oven while you prepare the sauce. (The recipe may be prepared to this point up to 15 minutes ahead of serving time.)

3. If the butter has browned, pour it out and add another 2 tablespoons butter to the pan. Add mushrooms, garlic, and green onion, turn heat to high, and sauté until the mushrooms begin to soften. Add sherry, bring to a boil, and reduce by half. Add cream, bring to a boil, and reduce to a thick sauce. Taste for seasoning, and correct if necessary.

4. Return chicken breasts to skillet to coat them with sauce. Serve topped with mushrooms and sauce.

Serves 4.

Duck Breasts With Wild Mushrooms and Cream Substitute duck breasts for the chicken, and fresh or dried wild mushrooms (cèpes, chanterelles, or shiitake) for the white ones. If you are using dried mushrooms, soak them in a little warm water until soft, and drain. Add the soaking liquid to the sauce along with the wine.

SAUTÉED FISH WITH PARSLEY-GARLIC SAUCE

> 4 fillets (4 to 6 oz each) firm, mild white fish
> 2 tablespoons olive oil
> 1 tablespoon chopped garlic
> 2 tablespoons chopped parsley
> ½ cup dry white wine
> ½ teaspoon freshly ground pepper
>   Salt to taste
>   Lemon juice to taste

1. Remove the fillets from the refrigerator at least 15 minutes before cooking. Let them come nearly to room temperature.

2. Have a warm serving platter ready. In a skillet large enough to hold the fillets in one layer, heat oil almost to the smoking point over medium-high heat. Add the fillets, skin side up. Cook until the edges are opaque, then turn and continue cooking until just done (when a skewer or toothpick easily penetrates the thickest part). Transfer cooked fillets to the platter.

3. Add garlic to the pan and sauté until it is soft and fragrant but not browned. Add parsley, wine, pepper, and a pinch of salt. Bring to a boil and reduce to less than half the original volume. Taste the sauce; it should be pleasantly tart and peppery. Add a little fresh lemon juice, if necessary. Pour the sauce over the fish and serve immediately.

Serves 4.

Step·by·Step

HOW TO MAKE A DEGLAZING SAUCE

Many sauces begin with the process of deglazing a roasting or sauté pan with wine. The instructions given here are based on Chicken Breasts With Sherry, Cream, and Mushrooms (see page 101).

1. *Sauté the lightly floured chicken breasts in the butter.*

2. *Breasts are done when they are lightly browned on both sides and firm to the touch. Transfer to warm plates.*

3. *Sauté the aromatic ingredients— mushrooms, garlic, and green onions—in the same skillet. As they cook, scrape up any bits of chicken or flour stuck to the pan.*

4. *Add wine and boil vigorously to reduce the volume and cook away the alcohol.*

5. *Add cream and reduce the sauce again. The cream provides the thickening power. Season the sauce to taste after reducing.*

PORT GRAVY FOR ROAST POULTRY

This recipe makes enough gravy for a good-sized roast chicken or duck. Triple the proportions for a turkey.

> *Pan drippings from a*
> *roasted bird*
> 1 *small onion, diced*
> *Half a rib of celery, diced*
> 1 *small carrot, diced*
> ½ *teaspoon fresh thyme leaves*
> 1 *bay leaf, crumbled*
> 3 *tablespoons flour*
> ½ *cup ruby or tawny port*
> 1½ *cups chicken stock*
> *Salt and pepper to taste*

1. Remove finished bird and rack, if used, from roasting pan. Cover bird with foil to keep it warm until serving time. Pour out and reserve drippings. (A heatproof glass measuring pitcher is helpful.)

2. Measure 2 tablespoons of fat from drippings and return to roasting pan. Add onion, celery, carrot, thyme, and bay leaf. Set pan over medium heat; lightly brown vegetables. Meanwhile, make a blond roux: Heat 2 table-spoons of remaining fat in a skillet (add butter, if necessary, to make 2 tablespoons). Stir in flour; cook over low heat until lightly colored.

3. Add port to roasting pan, turn heat to high, and bring wine to a boil, scraping up any drippings sticking to the pan. Skim off and discard remaining fat from reserved drippings. Add enough chicken stock to make 1½ cups. Add liquid to pan, stir in roux, and bring gravy to a boil, stirring frequently.

4. Season gravy to taste; simmer until thickened. Strain the finished gravy into the serving dish.

Makes 1½ cups.

Sherry Gravy For a less sweet, more delicate flavor, substitute the driest sherry you can find for the port in the above recipe. Use with roasted meats, especially veal or pork.

BEURRE ROUGE
Red-wine butter sauce

Wine butters make up another category of wine-based sauces. They use a reduction of wine and shallots or other onions to flavor a butter sauce. The concentrated acidity of the reduction performs a special magic: It keeps warm butter from "breaking" or separating, thus producing a smooth sauce, without the addition of egg yolks or starches.

Use this versatile sauce on meats, chicken, or mild fish—broiled, poached, or grilled.

> ½ cup dry red wine
> ¼ cup minced shallots
>   Pinch of white pepper
>   (optional)
> ½ cup cold butter, cut into
>   1-tablespoon pieces

1. Combine wine, shallots, and pepper (if used) in a small stainless steel, nonstick, or enameled saucepan (do not use an aluminum pan). Bring to a boil, reduce to a simmer, and cook until nearly all the liquid is gone and shallots are soft.

2. Remove half the reduction from pan. Remove the pan from the heat and stir in a piece of butter. Stir constantly until the butter is melted, then add another piece.

3. Return the pan to the gentlest possible heat. Continue adding butter, a piece at a time, stirring until each piece is nearly melted before adding the next. The sauce should have a creamy consistency. If the butter separates, the heat is too high; remove the pan from the heat and stir rapidly until an emulsion is formed.

4. Taste the sauce; it should be pleasantly tart. Add more of the reduction, if necessary, to make it more tart. Serve sauce immediately. (The remaining reduction can be stored in the refrigerator to make another batch of sauce.)

Makes ½ cup (4 servings).

Beurre Blanc Use white wine in place of the red wine to make *beurre blanc.* Serve it with delicately flavored fish.

Eggless Béarnaise Sauce Add chopped tarragon (either fresh or bottled in vinegar) to a red or white wine reduction to make a lighter version of Béarnaise sauce. Serve with grilled or roast beef, or with full-flavored fish.

Sautéed Chicken Breasts With Sherry, Cream, and Mushrooms (see page 101) is a fine complement to Chardonnay or other full-flavored white wines. The sauce lends itself to endless variations; in place of the mushrooms, try almonds or other nuts, artichoke hearts, or even a mixture of raisins and unsweetened coconut.

Amid antique cellar equipment, modern bottles from wineries across the country represent the range of wines now being made in the United States.

The Wines of America

California produces the vast majority of American wine—roughly four bottles out of five—but American wine does not begin and end with California. Each year it seems another vineyard springs up in a state that was never before considered a likely place to grow grapes for wine. This chapter examines American wine, with descriptions of the varieties grown here (pages 106–115) and an exploration, region by region, of the nation's wine-producing areas (pages 116–124).

THE RANGE OF AMERICAN WINES

The latest edition of the authoritative guide *The Wines of America* by Leon Adams lists 31 states other than California that produce "good wine": Alabama, Colorado, Connecticut, Florida, Georgia, Hawaii, Idaho, Illinois, Indiana, Kentucky, Maryland, Massachusetts, Michigan, Minnesota, Mississippi, Missouri, New Hampshire, New Jersey, New Mexico, New York, North and South Carolina, Ohio, Oregon, Pennsylvania, Rhode Island, Tennessee, Texas, Virginia, Washington, West Virginia, and Wisconsin (not to mention Ontario and British Columbia in Canada, or Baja California and several other Mexican states).

Perhaps the best way to classify American wines is by the types of grapes used to make them. The Eurasian vine species *Vitis vinifera* predominates in all vineyards west of the Rockies. The eastern wine industry was founded on the native American vine *V. labrusca*, but the French-American hybrids (see page 112) are now dominant, and vinifera has a small but important place in eastern viticulture.

The following is a catalog of the most important vinifera and hybrid grape varieties and their wines. Generic and semigeneric table wines and fortified wines are described on pages 114–115. The last section, beginning on page 116, is a geographic guide, with maps, to American vineyards, with notes on the best wines produced in each area.

Throughout this chapter, specific wines are cited as examples of each type. This is not meant to be a comprehensive review of American wines, however, and the absence of a particular wine does not imply that it is not worthy of inclusion here. Likewise, a wine that *is* mentioned here may not be to your taste. These recommendations are meant only as a guide to what is available; they shouldn't prevent you from trying another wine. Trust your own taste!

GRAPE VARIETIES AND VARIETAL WINES

As explained on pages 32–33, "varietal" wines are wines that are named for the variety of grape from which they are made. The following is a discussion of the varieties that produce the finest American wines. Red-wine grapes are listed first, followed by whites, with the most prestigious types heading each category.

PREMIUM VINIFERA REDS

Cabernet Sauvignon This grape is the standard-bearer for American red wines and the variety most responsible for the reputation California wines have gained worldwide. When grown in a suitable location, where there is a long growing season with warm but not hot summer days, the Cabernet grape makes full-flavored, aromatic wines, usually harsh and tannic when young, but improving in flavor, bouquet, and balance with age. The varietal aroma of Cabernet is herbaceous, sometimes with overtones of green olives, mint, or eucalyptus. The bouquet of mature Cabernets is often described as "cedary" or "woodsy."

Napa Valley Cabernets receive the most attention, but there are many fine examples from Sonoma County and the other coastal counties of California—from the northern region around Mendocino to the southern region near Santa Barbara. Eastern Washington already produces a lot of good—and some truly outstanding—Cabernet; production there is sure to increase. Plantings in other states are small, but they are also on the increase. Pioneering wineries in Virginia, Maryland, and other eastern states have produced a number of fine Cabernets.

Wineries producing good Cabernets number in the hundreds, but any list of the best would have to include the following: from California, Beaulieu, Beringer, Burgess, Caymus, Clos

du Bois, Clos du Val, Conn Creek, Freemark Abbey, Heitz, William Hill, Inglenook, Jordan, Louis Martini, Robert Mondavi, Joseph Phelps, Rutherford Hill, Sebastiani, Silver Oak, Spring Mountain, Stag's Leap Wine Cellars, Sterling, and Trefethen, among many others; from Washington, Chateau Ste. Michelle and Columbia; and from the eastern United States, Meredyth and Monticello in Virginia and Montbray in Maryland.

Most Cabernets need several years of bottle aging to develop the proper balance for drinking; far too many bottles are now drunk before they reach full maturity. Quite a few wineries are making two different wines out of Cabernet grapes—one in the traditional style that needs bottle aging and another (often under a second label) in a lighter, less tannic style that is more pleasant to drink at a younger age. These "second label" wines can be a real bargain, selling for half the price or less of the flagship wine and offering more immediate drinking pleasure. Beaulieu "Beau Tour," Glen Ellen "Proprietor's Reserve," Monterey Vineyard "Classic California Red," and the River Oaks brand from Clos du Bois are outstanding examples.

A few wineries make rosés from Cabernet grapes, and some of them are quite good. Simi makes an excellent example, a wine that preserves some of the distinctive aroma of the Cabernet grape but is lighter in body and lacks the tannin of the red version. Served chilled, Cabernet rosé is an excellent picnic or warm-weather wine. "White" Cabernet is similar, but generally less successful in capturing the Cabernet aroma.

Merlot Like Cabernet, Merlot is a grape native to Bordeaux, where it is usually blended with Cabernet varieties. It is similar to Cabernet in aroma and flavor, but it generally produces less tannic wines that are more drinkable when young. For this reason, much of the Merlot grown in California and Washington is used to "soften" Cabernet wines. Merlot is becoming increasingly popular as a varietal in its own right, largely because it offers good drinking at a younger age. Sterling was one of the first to produce a varietal Merlot and still makes one of the best. Rutherford Hill, Duckhorn, Louis Martini, and Gundlach-Bundschu are among other producers of fine Merlots.

Zinfandel The origin of this variety has long been a mystery, but recent research suggests that it is nearly identical to a southern Italian grape. Whatever its provenance, it is the most widely planted red-wine grape in California, accounting for about 10 percent of the total wine grape acreage.

For years, Zinfandel was a relatively obscure workhorse variety of grape. Beginning in the 1960s and 1970s, California winemakers tried just about everything with Zinfandel and several different styles emerged: the "claret style," which emulates Cabernet; the "late harvest" style of high-alcohol, sometimes sweet wines that approach the taste of port; and "Zinfandel Nouveau," made by the carbonic maceration method (see page 108).

Ridge has made a particular specialty of Zinfandel over the years. Its wines from such locations as York Creek in Napa County, Fiddletown in Amador County, and Paso Robles in San Luis Obispo County have set the standard for "claret-style" Zinfandels—wines that have the finesse as well as the strength of a Cabernet or Merlot. Lytton Springs Vineyard, which formerly supplied grapes to Ridge, now makes its own wine in a similar style. Burgess, Ravenswood, Kenwood, Dehlinger, Simi, Sausal, Dry Creek, and Storybook Mountain are among the other brands that produce full-bodied, distinctive Zinfandels. Monteviña and Sutter Home make typical Amador County Zinfandels, big and generous, full of ripe fruit but just short of raisiny. The portlike "late harvest" Zinfandels

An American regional flavor combination—Chesapeake Bay blue crabs and Maryland corn with wines from the nearby Piedmont area of Virginia.

from this area, which were all the rage a decade ago, seem to have fallen out of favor.

Throughout this era of experimentation with Zinfandel styles, many of the older "family" wineries of Sonoma and Napa just kept on making the same kind of wine. Today, many wine lovers are rediscovering the solid, dependable, thoroughly enjoyable Zinfandels of Martini, Krug, Parducci, Pedroncelli, Foppiano, Sebastiani, and Fetzer, to name a few. With all the current interest in "food wines," it was only a matter of time before this would happen.

"White" Zinfandel (which is usually a pale, salmon pink color) is one of the California wine industry's major success stories of the 1980s, exploding in popularity while demand for red wines remains static. The appeal of white Zinfandel is easy to understand. These wines are pretty to look at, easy to drink, typically a little bit sweet—in a word, friendly. The fresh, berrylike aromas of the grape come through nicely, even when the grapes are pressed immediately after crushing. The wines are generally inexpensive, because a buyer's market prevails in Zinfandel grapes. Sutter Home and Monteviña were among the originators of this style; they have been joined by dozens of others. Buehler makes a particularly nice version that is drier than most. Some wineries rush their white Zinfandels to the market a few months after harvest, not unlike Beaujolais Nouveau, and the trend seems to be catching on.

Pinot Noir In the Burgundy region of France, this variety of grape produces what some consider to be the finest red wines in the world. Certain sites in this country show promise of producing Pinot Noir grapes to rank with the best of those grown in Burgundy. Pinot Noir is difficult to grow and difficult to make into good wine. Winemakers are drawn to this variety, however, because the best wines are so good; soft, round, and beautifully scented, they go well with many kinds of food. The varietal aroma is reminiscent of cherries or plums and sweet spices; the best wines are medium bodied and relatively low in tannin, and most mature within five years of the vintage. The grape is a shy bearer, so the wines tend to be expensive.

Unfortunately, many Pinot Noir vineyards have been planted in unsuitable locations. Because it is an early-ripening variety, it has often been planted in the same areas as Cabernet Sauvignon; in this way, the Pinot could be picked in early September and would be fermented and into barrels before the Cabernet was harvested at the end of the month. But Pinot needs a cool growing season to produce good color, flavor, and aroma. In warm areas like the upper Napa Valley, the grapes ripen too quickly. They have plenty of sugar, but they lack the flavor that can only develop with slower ripening.

An additional problem with Pinot Noir is that there are a number of different clones, or subvarieties, with different characteristics. Some clones ripen earlier, some later; some have plenty of varietal character, others look the same but have little flavor. One clone has been widely mislabeled as Gamay Beaujolais. However, recent research has identified the best clones, and these dominate the newer plantings.

Despite all these difficulties, the right clone of Pinot Noir in the right place can make an excellent wine. The best California Pinots come from the vineyards of the Los Carneros viticultural area (Acacia, Beaulieu, Buena Vista, Carneros Creek), other cool parts of Sonoma County (Domaine Laurier, Mark West, Matanzas Creek), and various parts of the Central Coast (Calera, Chalone, Edna Valley, Firestone, Sanford). A few good Pinots are grown in the Finger Lakes region of New York. The most promising place of all may be the Willamette Valley of Oregon, which already produces a number of fine Pinots, including Adelsheim, Amity, Eyrie, Knudsen Erath, and Sokol Blosser.

Pinot Noir also makes good "white" wines, which are often labeled *Pinot Noir Blanc* or *Vin Gris*. These are more delicate wines than white Zinfandel, but their subtlety makes them better suited to a wide range of foods. The most successful white Pinots are sparkling wines. Many of the best California bruts contain up to half Pinot Noir, and a number of wineries make excellent blanc de noirs sparkling wines of 100 percent Pinot grapes.

Gamay, Gamay Beaujolais These names cover a confusing number of grape varieties, only one of which is the true grape of the Beaujolais region of France. Despite the ambiguity of the name, all these varieties make pleasant, light- to medium-bodied, fruity wines similar to Beaujolais. (Beaujolais, by the way, is a protected name for the wines of that region in France, and never appears by itself on an American label. Gamay Beaujolais is the legally accepted name of the grape grown here.) Gamays are versatile wines that are enjoyable with a wide variety of foods and taste especially good outdoors.

A few wineries make nouveau Gamay by a special process known as *carbonic maceration*, in which whole clusters of grapes are fermented without being crushed. The result is an intensely fruity wine with very little tannin. Charles Shaw and Sebastiani make excellent examples.

Petite Sirah and Syrah Despite the similarity of name, these two varieties are not related. Petite Sirah is widely grown, but it rarely makes first-rate wine by itself; varietal Petite Sirahs are often very tannic wines, some of them never coming around to perfect balance. However, Ridge, Stags' Leap Vintners, and Dry Creek make notable exceptions. These wines have plenty of fruit and body, but the tannins are kept at a reasonable level. With aging, they can become quite smooth; even when young, they are enjoyable with hearty, meaty fare. The varietal aroma is of berries, with a strong dose of black pepper that makes the wine a good match for strongly flavored foods like olives and garlic.

Syrah is a superior French variety from the Syrah region that is grown here in very limited quantity. The wine tastes like a refined version of Petite Sirah and has some of the same peppery quality. Joseph Phelps and Duxoup make the outstanding examples of the type.

OTHER VINIFERA REDS

Several other red vinifera varieties are grown, and in some cases they are bottled as varietals. Most of them are less distinctive than the "premium" varieties listed above, but in some cases they can make good varietal wines.

Barbera An Italian variety, this grape has the advantage of producing high acid in warmer areas. A few wineries, notably Louis Martini, Sebastiani, and Monterey Peninsula, make good varietal Barberas. These wines are medium bodied, with a vinous, slightly "tarry" aroma and good acidity, making them useful wines at the table.

Grenache This variety is native to southern France, where it is widely used in inexpensive, common reds. In California, it is used almost exclusively for rosés, some of which can be very pleasant. A few Washington producers make red Grenache wines, which have some of the black-pepper aroma of Petite Sirah but are much lighter in color and body.

Carignane Another southern French variety, Carignane is very productive and heat tolerant, but rarely, if ever, makes distinguished wine. It is mainly found in California jug wines.

Grignolino An Italian type, the Grignolino grape makes a light, pleasant wine of a pale, slightly orange color. Heitz makes both a red and a rosé Grignolino.

Ruby Cabernet This variety, a hybrid of Cabernet Sauvignon and Carignane that was developed at the University of California at Davis, preserves some of the aroma and flavor of Cabernet in the hotter interior valleys. A few wineries have bottled it as a varietal, but most of it goes into improving jug reds.

PREMIUM VINIFERA WHITES

Chardonnay This is the undisputed champion among the white wines of California. Like Cabernet Sauvignon, Chardonnay has brought California wines a worldwide reputation for quality. But California is not alone in producing fine wines from this variety; excellent examples are made in New York, Virginia, Washington, Oregon, and Idaho, among other states.

The varietal aroma of Chardonnay has been variously compared with apples, peaches, citrus fruits, melons, and honey, or combinations of these scents. However you describe it, it is an inviting aroma, which may be the key to its popularity. The flavor is fuller and richer than that of other whites. Barrel and bottle aging add complexity; if the wine has enough acidity, it can age seven to ten years or more.

There are regional and local differences in the quality of Chardonnay grapes, but an even more important factor may be the style of the winemaker. California Chardonnays are made in two or three styles. The key variables are the ripeness of the grapes (which determines the sugar level and thus the alcohol level of the wine) and the amount of barrel aging (see pages 21-22).

Some wineries, such as Beaulieu, prefer delicate, fruity Chardonnays, so they tend to pick the grapes at normal sugar levels and give their wines relatively little aging in oak. Charles Shaw, Lolonis, Almaden, Gallo, and some bottlings from Chateau St. Jean are among the California Chardonnays that emphasize the fruity quality. Most eastern Chardonnays, such as Hargrave from Long Island and Monticello and Meredyth from Virginia, tend toward the fruity style, as do the typical Oregon Chardonnays.

At the other extreme are the bigger, richer wines made from riper grapes, which are aged (and sometimes fermented) in small oak barrels to bring out the most intense flavors. Chalone, Edna Valley, Far Niente, Groth, Kenwood, Monticello (of the Napa Valley), Mount Eden, and Shafer are among the California examples of this style; a few are made elsewhere, such as Columbia and Yakima River Winery in Washington. This style became quite popular in California in the 1970s, as big, woody wines began to win competitive tastings. The best of these wines are delicious and well balanced, though intense in flavor. Some, however, are excessive, with alcohol levels up to 14 percent and strong wood flavors that dominate the wine.

Recently, there has been a tendency toward the middle of the road—a little less ripe, a little less emphasis on oak. The result is wines that are easier to enjoy with food. This is the predominant style of Chardonnay in California today. There are scores, perhaps hundreds, of fine examples of this type: Acacia, Bargetto, Burgess, Chateau Bouchaine, Chateau St. Jean, Clos du Bois, Firestone, Hacienda, Heitz, William Hill, Robert Mondavi, Joseph Phelps, Sequoia Grove, Sterling, Trefethen, ZD. These are just a few of the California Chardonnays that must be ranked among the most prestigious American white wines.

Sauvignon Blanc, Fumé Blanc These are two names for the same grape, one of the most popular in California in recent years. It is native to France's Loire Valley and to Bordeaux, where it is typically blended with Semillon for both dry and sweet wines. In California and Washington, it produces a distinctive, strongly scented wine with an herbaceous or "grassy" aroma, medium body, and good acidity, making it a good wine to serve with assertive foods, such as garlic, fresh coriander, and green

The firm acidity of most white wines, such as this Sauvignon Blanc–Semillon blend, makes them ideal partners for an assortment of caviars—golden (whitefish), red (salmon), and black (sturgeon).

peppers. Fumé Blanc is a fairly recent name, coined by Robert Mondavi in the 1960s. In the Loire Valley, the grape is known as Blanc Fumé; Mondavi reversed the two words and found the wine easier to sell under the new name. Whether consumers found "Sauvignon" hard to pronounce or just preferred the style of the wine Mondavi made (which is dry, with a pronounced varietal aroma and a touch of wood from barrel aging) isn't clear, but the name caught on. Now about half of the varietal wines of this type are labeled Fumé Blanc, although most also have the name Sauvignon Blanc somewhere on the label.

Like Chardonnay, Sauvignon Blanc can be made in a number of styles. Some winemakers emphasize the grassy aroma and flavor, others produce a less aggressively fruity wine. A few ferment their Sauvignon Blanc in oak, as with a Chardonnay, but most prefer shorter barrel aging, just enough to take the rough edges off the wine. Some wineries prefer the name Fumé Blanc, and bottle the wine in a slope-shouldered bottle to suggest a similarity to the herbaceous wines of the Loire, while others use a clear, straight-sided bottle to suggest the lighter, milder flavors of a white Bordeaux. It would be convenient if the name and bottle shape were reliable guides to style, but there are a lot of variations from this formula; each winery ultimately chooses the style, label, and bottle it likes.

There are hundreds of wineries now making Sauvignon Blanc or Fumé Blanc. Among the best in the grassy-varietal style are the Sauvignons of Beaulieu, Glen Ellen, Grand Cru, Kenwood, and Silverado, and the Chateau Ste. Michelle Fumé. Carmenet and Carneros Creek demonstrate the benefits of barrel-aging Sauvignon Blanc; a noticeable flavor of oak balances the assertive quality of the grape. Among the better examples of the milder, less grassy style are the Fumés of Chateau St. Jean, Christian Brothers, Deloach, Charles LeFranc, Charles Shaw, and the Sterling Sauvignon.

Semillon (also known as Chevrier Blanc) This is the other great white Bordeaux variety, usually blended with Sauvignon Blanc for both dry and sweet wines. In California and Washington, it is sometimes bottled as a varietal, sometimes in a blend with Sauvignon. The varietal character is somewhat herbaceous like Sauvignon, but with the additional aroma of ripe figs. Wente Bros.

pioneered the variety in California and still make a popular version. Vichon makes an excellent proprietary blend, called "Chevrignon," of roughly equal parts of Semillon and Sauvignon Blanc. Columbia, Chateau Ste. Michelle, and Adelsheim make excellent wines from Semillon grapes grown in eastern Washington.

Riesling, Johannisberg Riesling, White Riesling These are all names for the same grape, one of the noblest varieties in the world. In Germany and Alsace, it is known simply as Riesling; in California, that name is allowed for other grapes as well, and the true variety is known as White Riesling or Johannisberg Riesling (after Johannisberg on the Rhine, one of Germany's finest vineyard sites). White Riesling is the preferable name, and the only one allowed by Oregon law.

At its best, Riesling has a delightful flowery-apricot aroma and a light, refreshing flavor. It can be made dry, but most people seem to prefer it with a bit of sweetness. The drier versions go quite well with seafood, especially shellfish. Sweeter Rieslings are better just by themselves, or with fruit.

The Riesling grape needs a long, cool growing season to show its best qualities; otherwise the wine can be flat or bitter. Perhaps the best conditions in the country for Riesling are in western Oregon and Washington. Amity, Hillcrest, Hinman, and Tualatin in Oregon, and Arbor Crest, Chateau Ste. Michelle, and Columbia in Washington are among the producers of outstanding Rieslings in the Northwest. Riesling also does quite well in the Finger Lakes; Glenora, Heron Hill, McGregor, Vinifera Wine Cellars, and Hermann Wiemer make good versions, including some of the sweet, late-harvest type. Fully ripe Riesling from the warmer areas often makes a slightly bitter-tasting wine with a "piney" aroma.

In California, Riesling has been problematic. The areas that produce other fine wines are often too warm for good Rieslings, other than the late-harvest type. The best California Rieslings come from the coolest regions—mostly the coastal valleys from Monterey south—or from wineries that take care to pick extra-early. These wines tend to be on the sweet side. Bargetto, Felton-Empire, Firestone, and Jekel are among the makers of fine Central Coast Rieslings. Trefethen makes a Napa Valley Riesling that confounds the rules—a dry, perfectly balanced wine that goes quite well with roast pork.

A few California wineries make wines labeled simply "Riesling." These are not the same as the white Riesling; they are made of Sylvaner grapes, a lesser German variety. A totally unrelated French grape is known in California as "Grey Riesling" but bears no resemblance to Riesling.

Gewürztraminer This grape has perhaps the most distinctive varietal aroma of all—it is intensely spicy and flowery. *(Gewürz* is German for spicy; *Traminer* is the name of the parent variety, of which this variety is a particularly spicy clone.) In Europe, it is grown on both sides of the Rhine, in France's Alsace region and in Germany; the Alsatian wines are dry and intense, while the German versions are lower in alcohol and typically a little sweet. American Gewürztraminers fall somewhere in the middle; they are usually a little sweet, but fuller bodied than the German type.

Like Riesling, the Gewürztraminer grape needs a cool location to do its best; otherwise it will produce a wine that is low in acid and disappointingly flat. Oregon and Washington show promise of producing good Gewürztraminers, but so far the best examples are coming from cooler parts of California. The Anderson Valley of Mendocino County produces more than its share of good ones, especially those of Navarro and Edmeades. The Central Coast is also a good place for Gewürztraminer; Firestone makes an excellent one in Santa Barbara County, and several wineries have made good wines from grapes from the Tepusquet Vineyard near Santa Maria. Claiborne & Churchill is a new label to watch from the Edna Valley area. The best winemakers can make excellent wines even in warmer areas. Phelps Napa Valley Gewürztraminer and the Clos du Bois Alexander Valley "Early Harvest" bottlings are two consistent examples of fine wines grown where the experts say it is too warm for this variety.

With its distinctive aroma and flavor, Gewürztraminer is frequently recommended to go with highly seasoned foods, from ham and sausages to curries and Chinese foods. But it is quite an adaptable wine, and it would be a shame to serve it only with "problem" foods. It can be enjoyed whenever the occasion calls for a wine with a lot of character.

Pinot Blanc This grape hails from Burgundy, where it is sometimes used in blends with Chardonnay. It is similar to Chardonnay, but less aromatic. Most of it goes into sparkling wine blends, but a few wineries, especially in California's Monterey County, produce it as a varietal table wine. Ventana, Chalone, Jekel, and Mirassou make varietal Monterey Pinot Blancs (Mirassou under the semigeneric name "White Burgundy") that are less costly alternatives to their Chardonnays.

OTHER VINIFERA WHITES

Chenin Blanc This is the white counterpart of Zinfandel: productive, widely planted, adaptable to many localities and styles. It produces light, fruity wines that are usually fermented cold to accentuate the fruit. Most Chenin Blancs are slightly sweet, and they are very popular. Robert Mondavi introduced the fruity, cold-fermented style when he was at Charles Krug, then brought it with him to his own winery. Wente makes a popular version under the brand name "Le Blanc de Blancs." This style goes well with lighter meals and picnics, and many people like it with just about everything. A few wineries, notably Dry Creek and Villa Mt. Eden, make a dry, barrel-aged Chenin Blanc, a sort of "poor man's Chardonnay."

Muscats and Malvasia Bianca

This is a loose grouping of varieties, some related, some not, but all with a strong grapy aroma familiar to anyone who has eaten Muscat grapes. When made light and sweet, Muscat wines can be refreshing and delicious, especially with fresh fruit desserts. This type goes under several names: Muscat Blanc, Muscat Canelli, Moscato di Canelli, Moscato Amabile, and a number of similar proprietary names. Mondavi, Krug, Robert Pecota, Estrella River, and Washington's Tucker Cellars make good examples. Martini makes a delicious, slightly sparkling Moscato Amabile—unfortunately, it is available only at the winery.

A few wineries make fortified "liqueur" wines from Muscat types (see "Fortified or 'Dessert' Wines," page 115).

French Colombard is mainly a bulk variety, valuable because it produces good acidity in warm areas, such as the San Joaquin Valley. As a varietal, it makes clean, fruity, balanced (if unremarkable) wine. Almaden makes a good example in fifths and jugs. Gallo Chablis Blanc could probably qualify as a varietal French Colombard.

Thompson Seedless is a name never seen on a label (except as a joke), but a lot of these grapes go into Central Valley jug white wines. The Thompson Seedless is California's triple-threat grape—it can be eaten at the table, dried for raisins, or made into wine. If it has a varietal aroma, it is vaguely grapelike.

FRENCH-AMERICAN HYBRIDS

Dozens of varieties of French-American hybrid grapes (see page 11) have been planted experimentally in the eastern states. Of these, a few are beginning to be recognized as having distinct varietal character. Most hybrids are known by the name of the hybridizer and a number, but several have become known by more conventional-sounding names that are starting to appear as varietal wine labels. (For instance, Baco No. 1 is known as Baco Noir, Seyve-Villard 5276 as Seyval Blanc.) Baco Noir is the most visible example among the reds, and it can make a fine wine—round, soft, and easily drinkable like a good Gamay or lighter Pinot Noir, but with a touch of the black-pepper aroma of Petite Sirah. It is an important variety in New York, Michigan, and several other eastern states. Chancellor is another good red hybrid; its wines have more "backbone" of tannin and body, a little like Zinfandel. Chambourçin is not widely known, but some experts consider it among the best hybrid reds. Other hybrid red varietals include Foch (or Maréchal Foch), Leon Millot, De Chaunac, and Chelois.

Seyval Blanc is the most successful white hybrid on the market. Some have compared it to Chardonnay, and it does have some of the same apple and citrus-peel aromas of that variety, but it generally makes lighter, more delicate wine. Cayuga is a popular variety in the Finger Lakes, and has a pleasant apple aroma and flavor. Vignoles has a delicate fruity-floral aroma resembling Riesling, while the related Ravat Blanc is almost a caricature of the same aromas, with overtones of papaya and other tropical fruits. Aurore (Aurora on some labels), Vidal Blanc, and Rayon d'Or are other white hybrids that are beginning to appear as varietals.

The selection of hybrid varieties available to growers is steadily expanding. According to Philip Wagner, an active nurseryman who is mainly responsible for introducing the hybrids in this country, grape hybridization is "an ongoing process with an endless future." New varieties are constantly being developed, although each takes 10 to 20 years of experimental planting before it can become commercially important. Growers, winemakers, and consumers can look forward to an increasing number of choices among hybrids in the decades to come.

Wagner also cautions against assuming that varietal labeling is always the best way to go. As is the case with vinifera wines, a skillful winemaker can blend wines with different characteristics to produce a wine with better balance than any of its component varietal wines. If we as consumers can avoid preconceptions and instead judge each wine on its own merits, winemakers can concentrate their efforts on making the best possible wines from the grapes available.

Sweet Wines and the "Noble Mold"

Most fungus organisms are a problem in the vineyard, damaging either leaves or fruit, or both. A bad infection of a particular mold known as "bunch rot" or "gray rot" just before harvest can destroy a vintage; the moldy flavor of the grapes carries over to the wine. However, given perfect conditions (a narrow range of temperature and humidity), the very same organism, *Botrytis cinerea*, can be beneficial.

Every few years, the perfect conditions—a little rainfall or a day of high humidity, followed by several days of dry weather—occur when the grapes are fully ripe, and the ignoble gray rot is transformed into what the French call *pourriture noble* and the Germans *Edelfäule*, or "the noble rot." The grower gambles and leaves the grapes on the vine later than usual, and the botrytis goes to work. As the mold grows on the surface of the grapes, it softens the skin to the point at which the moisture evaporates but the sugar and flavor remain. The result is an exceedingly ugly, shriveled bunch of grapes, but inside is an intense natural concentrate of grape juice, with up to twice the sugar content of normal juice. By selecting these bunches from the regular harvest, the winemaker can make a very special wine—one that is sweet and intense, overflowing with natural varietal flavor.

In Europe, the most famous wines of this type are the great French Sauternes and the German *beerenauslese* and *trockenbeerenauslese* wines (the last term means, literally, "dryberry-selected-late-harvest"). In certain American vineyards, botrytis occasionally affects the same grape varieties: Semillon, Sauvignon Blanc, Riesling, and Gewürztraminer. The resulting "late-harvest" wines compare favorably with their European counterparts.

It is possible to make late-harvest wines without benefit of botrytis simply by leaving the grapes on the vine longer; however, this tends to produce raisiny flavors. The beauty of botrytis is that it concentrates the natural, ripe flavors without a hint of raisin flavor. Most wines made from "botrytized" (botrytis-affected) grapes make some mention of it on the label.

Riesling is the most commonly affected variety, if such a rare occurrence can be called common. Chateau St. Jean has made a specialty of sweet, botrytized late-harvest Rieslings, as has Freemark Abbey, with its "Edelwein Gold" brand. Joseph Phelps has an experimental plot of Scheurebe, a related German variety, which has also produced wine of the same type. Botrytized Rieslings and Gewürztraminers have also been made in Monterey County and elsewhere on the central coast, and in eastern Washington and the Finger Lakes region in New York.

Sauvignon Blanc and Semillon are less frequently affected by botrytis, but when they are, the results are equally spectacular. Monticello's 1982 "Chateau M" was an outstanding recent example of a sweet Sauvignon Blanc, and vanished from the market almost immediately.

These very special wines will always be in short supply, so they are necessarily expensive. Not only do they demand extra labor, for the bunches must be hand-selected and carefully inspected, but only about half as much wine can be produced per acre of vineyard. Also, the conditions for the growth of the noble mold do not occur every year. Fortunately, most wineries that make these sweet wines bottle them in halfbottles, making it twice as likely that you will get a chance to try one. Since these sweet wines are meant to be sipped in small quantities, a halfbottle is plenty for most occasions.

PRONUNCIATION GUIDE

Many names of grape varieties come from the French, German, or Italian. Here is a slightly simplified guide to typical American pronunciation of these names. Syllables marked with an asterisk end in a typically French silent nasal sound, as if you were saying "long" without the final "g." Stress falls on the italicized syllables.

Baco Noir   *bah*-ko *nwahr*

Barbera   bar-*bare*-a

Cabernet Sauvignon   kab-er-*nay so*-vee-nyon*

Carignane   *car*-een-nyan

Chardonnay   *shar*-done-nay

Chenin Blanc   *shen*-an *blon**

Gamay Beaujolais   *gam*-may *bo*-zho-lay

Gewürztraminer   geh-*vertz*-tra-*mee*-ner

Grenache Rosé   gre-*nosh* ro-*zay*

Grignolino   gree-nyo-*lee*-no

Johannisberg Riesling   yo-*hohn*-iss-berg *rees*-ling

Malvasia Bianca   mal-*vase*-ee-ah bee-*ahn*-kah

Merlot   mare-*low*

Pinot Blanc   *pee*-no *blon**

Pinot Noir   *pee*-no *nwahr*

Sauvignon Blanc   *so*-vee-nyon* *blon**

Semillon   *sem*-me-yon*

Seyval Blanc   *Say*-vahl *blon**

Vignoles   vee-*nyoll*

Vin Gris   van* gree

Vin Rosé   van* ro-*zay*

113

Generic and Semigeneric Wines

As is explained on page 34, many American wines take their names from the (sometimes Anglicized) names of European wines. These *semigeneric* names, which properly refer only to specific wines from specific places in Europe, have become firmly established in the American wine business, and it will probably be many more years before they are abolished in favor of true generic names like "red table wine."

Burgundy is the most common red semigeneric label. It usually implies a dry red wine, but some burgundies are noticeably sweet. *Chablis* can be either sweet or dry, depending on the maker, while *Rhine* is almost always sweet. *Chianti* was formerly more common on California labels, but is now almost extinct.

Claret is the least objectionable name of this type, because it is not a place name; rather, it is the traditional English name for the red wines of Bordeaux, derived from the French *clairet*, a general term for a light-colored red wine. "Claret" is enjoying a return to fashion in California as a curious result of recent changes in varietal labeling laws. Under the old laws, a blend of 60 percent Cabernet Sauvignon and 40 percent Merlot (a blend typical of a great Bordeaux) could be labeled Cabernet Sauvignon. Such a blend would be more complex in flavor and somewhat softer and more drinkable when young than a straight Cabernet. The new laws, however, require at least 75 percent of the named variety for a varietal label. Wineries have the option of spelling out the exact varietal percentages on the label, but some have simply opted for the label "Claret" and let the wines speak for themselves. Ridge Vineyards has revived the label for some of its "field blend" Zinfandels—wines from vineyards planted to a blend of varieties, made in a "claret" style.

True Generics A number of wineries have made the move from semigeneric names to truly generic labels, and they are to be applauded. Phelps and Chateau St. Jean call their generics Vin Rouge and Vin Blanc. Fetzer Premium Red and Premium White and Robert Mondavi Red, White, and Rosé are other good examples of honest, straightforward generic labeling. Trefethen "Eshcol" Red and White and Taylor "Lake Country" Red, White, and Pink are examples of another good approach, in which a proprietary name is added to the generic labels.

Sparkling Wines

American "Champagne," or more properly, sparkling wine, runs the gamut from the inexpensive bulk-process wines served on airlines to fine méthode champenoise wines made from choice varieties. (See pages 23-25 for a discussion of the technique and terminology of sparkling wines.) Altogether it constitutes the fastest-growing segment of the American wine industry.

The great majority of sparkling wines produced in California are made by either bulk process or transfer process. Gallo is by far the leader in quantity, producing about half of the state's total output, primarily with its "André" label. Weibel is another large house that sells good bulk-process sparkling wines, under the "Weibel" and "Stanford" labels and under numerous private labels for stores and restaurants. Christian Brothers' bulk-process sparkling wines are quite good. Paul Masson and Almaden are major producers of transfer-process wines. Almaden's Blanc de Blanc and Weibel's Chardonnay Brut are among the best examples of the potential for quality in transfer-process wines.

At the top of the price range for California sparkling wines are the méthode champenoise wines, the best of which approach the quality of real Champagne. Until the 1970s, three specialty wineries—Korbel, Hanns Kornell, and Schramsberg—produced most of the Champagne-method wines in the state, although a few others, such as Beaulieu, Mirassou, and Sonoma Vineyards, made some sparkling wines. In the 1970s, the potential demonstrated by these wineries and a few others attracted the Champagne house of Moët et Chandon to establish Domaine Chandon in the Napa Valley. They were followed a few years later by Piper-Heidsieck with its Piper-Sonoma label. Both are now among the top sparkling wines in the state. Several other Champagne houses have bought vineyards in California in recent years. Look for Roederer wines from Mendocino County and Deutz wines from San Luis Obispo County in the years to come, as well as new wines from Spanish sparkling-wine producers.

Along with the infusion of capital from overseas have come a number of new sparkling-wine producers. Chateau St. Jean makes excellent brut and blanc de blancs and produces sparkling wines for other labels, including Sebastiani. Culbertson, in San Diego County, began winning awards with its first releases. About a dozen new California sparkling wines will come onto the market during the mid-1980s, and the early indications are that they will be very good.

New York State sparkling wine has a decades-long reputation for quality. The wines are typically made from a blend of labrusca and hybrid grapes, but they have almost no "foxy" aroma. Washington and Oregon are also starting to produce sparkling wines; in fact, the coolest parts of the Northwest may be ideal for producing low-sugar, high-acid grapes—the basic requirement for good sparkling wine. It would not be surprising if a French Champagne firm decided before long to settle in Oregon.

Fortified or "Dessert" Wines

As American wines come of age, most of the attention is being focused on table wines. Yet until the late 1960s, the majority of California wine was of the "fortified" or "dessert" type. Both of these terms are a little misleading, but they refer to the whole category of wines with more than 14 percent alcohol: sherry, port, Madeira, Tokay, muscatel, angelica, and a smattering of varietally labeled wines, mainly of the Muscat type.

Like the semigeneric table wines, many of these high-alcohol wines take their names from European models. Here are some of the most common types:

Port is a red wine "fortified" by the addition of brandy at a carefully calculated time during the fermentation. The alcohol in the brandy kills the yeasts, stopping the fermentation when a substantial portion of the natural sugar remains. The resulting wine is sweet and strong, with 18 to 20 percent alcohol. With some aging in the barrel or bottle, it can be delicious, a perfect after-dinner companion to firm cheeses and nuts.

"Port" is a shortened form of Oporto, the name of a Portuguese seaport from which the original version is still shipped. Like their Portuguese models, California ports are made in three distinct styles. Vintage port is wine of a single vintage, bottled at an age of two years, and generally needing several more years of aging in the bottle. Ruby port is also bottled young, but it is usually meant for immediate consumption. Tawny ports are aged in barrels for many years, during which they become smoother and less fruity and faded in color, as the name implies. White port is a similar wine made from white grapes; it is not remarkable.

Port can be made from any red grapes, and it can come from areas as diverse as California's cool coastal vineyards, the hot Central Valley, or the foothills of the Sierra. A few wineries use authentic Portuguese varieties, chiefly Tinta Madeira and Souzão. Ficklin Tinta Port has been the industry standard for many years, but it has recently been joined at the top by wines from Quady, J. W. Morris, and Woodbury, which use premium table-wine varietals. Most of the largest California wineries, such as Gallo, Italian Swiss Colony, Almaden, Paul Masson, and Christian Brothers, make a line of ports, some of them quite good.

Sherry is another wine patterned after an Old World classic. The name is the English form of Jerez, the name of a town in southwest Spain that is the center of production of a distinctive family of fragrant, earthy, golden wines. Unfortunately, most California sherry does not come close to the original in quality.

Sherry is an intentionally oxidized wine. Where most winemakers try to avoid oxidation by keeping barrels full and tightly sealed, the sherry maker encourages oxidation by aging the wine in half-empty barrels. In California, dry white wines destined to become sherry are fortified with brandy, then generally "baked" (aged in heated rooms) to speed up the aging process. Older and younger wines are blended to maintain consistency of style, and the wine is typically sweetened before bottling with a reserve of very sweet wine.

A few California sherries are completely dry, but most are sweetened to some degree. The driest are labeled *pale dry, cocktail,* or sometimes *fino,* which is the Spanish term; the sweetest are usually called *cream sherry.* Between these two are the somewhat sweet wines labeled *dry, medium dry,* or *golden.* These terms are not consistent from one house to another, however.

Dry and medium sherries are mainly served as apéritifs, perhaps with toasted nuts and olives. Sweet sherry is usually sipped after dinner, like a liqueur. Sherry is often called for in cooking, in which case it is best to use the driest one available unless the recipe is for a sweet dish.

Muscat varieties make fine fortified wines, sweet and aromatic. Beaulieu Muscat de Frontignan and Beringer Malvasia Bianca are excellent examples. A newcomer, Quady Orange Muscat "Essencia," may be the best of all. *Muscatel* is an honorable name in Europe, used for a type of sweet, sometimes fortified wine made from Muscat varieties; but here the term usually describes a cheap, undistinguished high-alcohol wine.

Other fortified wines that take their names from European types include Madeira, Marsala, and Tokay. Madeira is a "baked" wine similar to sherry; in fact, the California "baked" sherry process is almost identical to the technique used in making fortified wines on the island of Madeira. Marsala is sweetened with boiled-down must, giving it a caramelized flavor. It takes its name from a Sicilian specialty. Tokay is both a grape variety and a wine, although neither bears much resemblance to the world-famous sweet Tokaj wines of Hungary. In fact, California "Tokay" is more likely to be a blend of various fortified wines than a varietal wine made from Tokay grapes.

Angelica is a type of fortified wine unique to California, made by adding brandy to unfermented must. The resulting wine (if it can really be called wine) can be delicious. Traditionally, angelica was aged like tawny port or sherry to produce an after-dinner sipping wine. Domaine Chandon has introduced a version called "Panache" from its sparkling-wine stock, which they recommend drinking as an apéritif, over ice with a twist of lemon. It tastes especially good outdoors. Mark West Vineyards has imitated this wine right down to the label design with its "Angelique," which is also quite good.

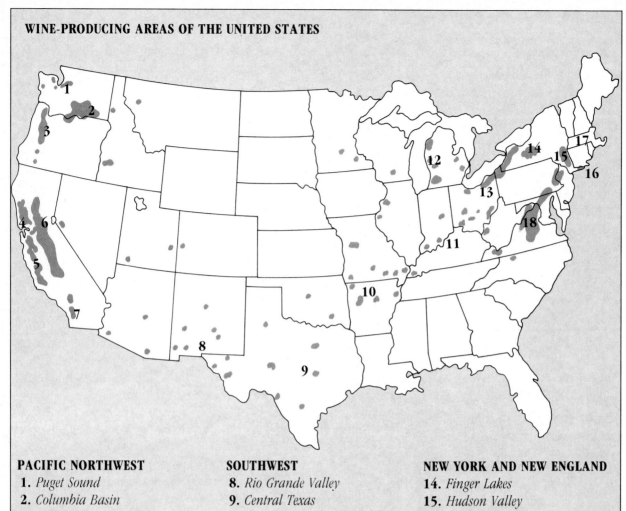

WINE-PRODUCING AREAS OF THE UNITED STATES

PACIFIC NORTHWEST
1. *Puget Sound*
2. *Columbia Basin*
3. *Willamette Valley*

CALIFORNIA
4. *North Coast*
5. *Central Coast*
6. *Central Valley and Sierra Foothills*
7. *South Coast*

SOUTHWEST
8. *Rio Grande Valley*
9. *Central Texas*

MIDWEST AND GREAT LAKES
10. *Ozark Plateau*
11. *Ohio Valley*
12. *Western Michigan*
13. *Lake Erie Shore*

NEW YORK AND NEW ENGLAND
14. *Finger Lakes*
15. *Hudson Valley*
16. *Long Island*
17. *Southern New England*

MID-ATLANTIC STATES
18. *Piedmont*

THE VINEYARDS OF AMERICA

American wines are generally identified by type and by brand name, but the finest wines of Europe are almost always identified with a particular *place*. The wines of Château Lafite-Rothschild always come from the same vineyard; the winemaker, regardless of skill, cannot make the same wine with grapes from another source. Chambertin, Montrachet, Hermitage, Schloss Johannisberg, and scores of other famous wines are identified by the place where the grapes were grown. Over the centuries, growers and winemakers have found these particularly favored spots where the sun, soil, and climate are perfect for each grape variety. Plant the same variety a few miles away, however, and it may make ordinary or even poor wine.

By comparison with the wine-growing regions of the Old World, American vineyards and the American wine industry are still quite young. The quality of the best American wines is all the more remarkable when one considers that we have had only a few decades, just a few years in some cases, to find the best locations for each grape and vice versa. As growers and winemakers get better at matching grape varieties to local conditions, we will undoubtedly see further advances in quality.

Here, then, is a guide to the best vineyard districts of America, the types of wine they produce best today, and what to look for in the future.

CALIFORNIA

California produces the majority of American wine, almost all of it from vinifera grapes, the state's moderate climate being the closest in North America to that of the grape's ancestral home in the Mediterranean.

The vineyard districts of California can be roughly classified into the North Coast, Central Coast, Central Valley, Sierra foothills, and South Coast. Not all of the "coastal" areas actually border on the ocean, but they all share the moderating influence of ocean air. The interior can be much hotter in summer, making it less suited to fine table wines.

In discussing the wine-growing areas, it is convenient to use the "heat-summation" scale developed in 1944 at the University of California at Davis. Professors Maynard Amerine and Albert J. Winkler distinguished five regions, based on the average daily temperature during the growing season. Region I, consisting of the coolest areas where grapes will ripen reliably, occurs closest to the coast, where marine air keeps summer temperatures low. Late-ripening varieties like Cabernet Sauvignon and Sauvignon Blanc may not ripen fully every year in this region, but early-season varieties like Pinot Noir show their best qualities here. Region II is warmer, but still tempered by ocean breezes and fog. Most varieties will ripen fully and make good wines in this region. Region III shows less marine influence, with correspondingly higher summer temperatures. The early-season grapes that do so well in Region I ripen too quickly here, giving good sugar readings but producing wines lacking in flavor. Late-ripening varieties such as Zinfandel and Petite Sirah are better suited to Region III conditions. Region IV includes interior areas with only slight cooling from ocean breezes, and Region V covers the hottest interior valleys. Region IV is the practical limit for fine table wines, but a lot of jug wine is made from Region V grapes.

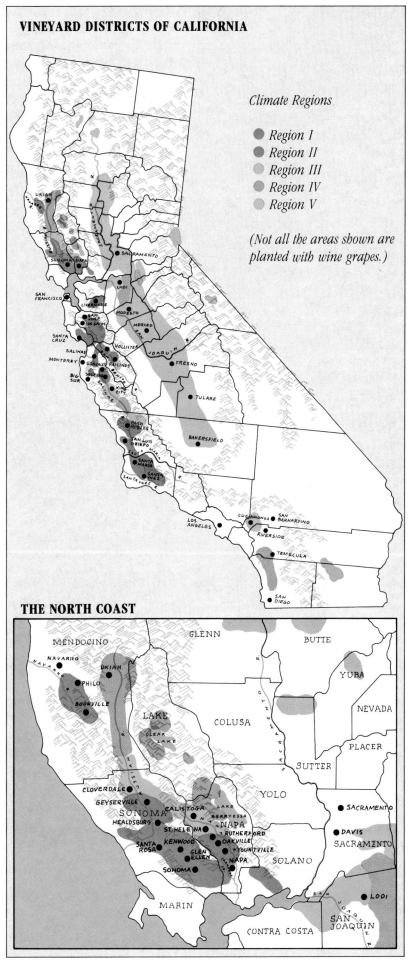

VINEYARD DISTRICTS OF CALIFORNIA

Climate Regions

● Region I
● Region II
● Region III
● Region IV
● Region V

(Not all the areas shown are planted with wine grapes.)

THE NORTH COAST

117

The North Coast

When a visitor to San Francisco talks about "the wine country," he or she almost always means Napa and Sonoma counties. These two counties offer the highest concentration of wineries and fine wines in the country. Together with Mendocino County, the landlocked Lake County to the north and relatively small acreage in Solano and Contra Costa counties, they make up the North Coast. Climates in this district range from too cold and foggy to ripen grapes to a few semiarid spots too hot to grow good grapes. Between these extremes lie thousands of acres of choice vineyards, with the ideal combination of mild winters, warm summer days, and cool summer nights for growing fine grapes.

The Napa Valley viticultural area encompasses not only the valley itself, but the surrounding mountains and even a couple of neighboring valleys. The southern end, which includes the Carneros viticultural area and the Napa Valley as far north as Yountville, is Region I, and it produces fine Pinot Noir and Chardonnay. The Stag's Leap area, although technically Region I, is at the warm end, and produces fine Cabernet. North of Yountville, Region II begins, and it is here that Cabernet and its relatives come into their own. The west side of the valley from Oakville to near St. Helena is planted almost solidly with Cabernet, producing some of California's most prestigious wines, including the Heitz Martha's Vineyard, Beaulieu Private Reserve, and Robert Mondavi Reserve. The rest of the valley, including the Region III area around Calistoga, is planted with a wide mix of varieties. The hillsides around the valley mainly produce intense Zinfandel, Cabernet, and Chardonnay wines.

The Los Carneros viticultural area straddles the Napa-Sonoma county line where the ridge separating the two valleys nearly meets the San Francisco Bay. This is cool Region I, the perfect spot for Pinot Noir and Chardonnay. On the Napa side, Acacia, Carneros Creek, and the new Chateau Bouchaine are making outstanding wines from this area. One of the most famous Carneros names is not a winery but a vineyard, Winery Lake, which has been known to sell grapes to a dozen or more wineries each year, all of which proudly display the name of the vineyard on the label. On the Sonoma side, Buena Vista has moved nearly all of its operation from the town of Sonoma to Carneros, where it produces almost its entire line. Buena Vista is even growing good Cabernet in Carneros, which was previously thought to be too cool for this variety.

Sonoma County lies closer to the ocean than Napa, and thus is generally cooler. It offers at least as wide a range of growing conditions as Napa, but unlike its neighbor, it is divided into a number of smaller viticultural areas under the new laws (see "Source of Grapes," page 34).

The Sonoma Valley viticultural area in the southeastern part of the county is a cool Region I. The appellation includes the Sonoma Valley proper, a major part of the Carneros district, and the narrow valley northwest of Sonoma, including the towns of Glen Ellen and Kenwood. Sebastiani, Hacienda, and Gundlach-Bundschu concentrate on Sonoma Valley grapes; other wineries such as Chateau St. Jean, Kenwood, and Glen Ellen use grapes from other parts of the county as well as local grapes. Hanzell, which pioneered the use of French oak barrels for Pinot Noir and Chardonnay, lies in the hills north of Sonoma, as do the Monte Rosso Vineyard (whose grapes go into some of Martini's best wines) and the new Carmenet vineyard and winery.

The tall ridge known as Sonoma Mountain also lies within the Sonoma Valley appellation, but some growers there prefer the more narrow identity of Sonoma Mountain. Matanzas Creek Winery is an outstanding producer of Sonoma Mountain wines. West of Sonoma Mountain is Green Valley, an area that produces fine Pinot Noirs and Chardonnays (Dehlinger, Iron Horse, and Domaine Laurier are good examples).

A little north is the Russian River Valley, which is Region I up to Healdsburg. Above Healdsburg lie Dry Creek and Alexander valleys, both Region II. The Dry Creek area produces some exceptional Zinfandels and Chardonnays, and Alexander Valley particularly excels in Chardonnays and Cabernets. Jordan, Alexander Valley Vineyard, Simi, and Clos du Bois are among the many wineries making fine Alexander Valley wines. The northeastern corner of Sonoma County, above Geyserville, is the warmest, a Region III.

Sonoma County should prove an interesting testing ground for the new viticultural-area system. Some Sonoma growers and winemakers have chosen a strong local identification, joining their reputation to that of the district. Others think that the partitioning is premature, and that there is more to be gained from promoting the county as a whole. Consumer response will probably be the key. In a little over a decade, Alexander Valley has already shown itself to be a salable name, and others will probably follow.

Mendocino County vineyards used to be limited to the warmer (Region III) eastern side of the county, particularly the Redwood Valley area. Fetzer and Parducci are consistent producers of solid, enjoyable, reasonably priced wines in the eastern half, and newcomers like Lolonis and McDowell Valley are adding to the area's reputation. Much of the county's recent growth has been in the cooler Anderson Valley to the west. This area may be one of the best in the state for Gewürztraminer and Riesling, and perhaps Pinot Noir and Chardonnay as well. Navarro, Husch, Edmeades, and Pepperwood Springs are names to look for.

Lake County lies north of Napa and east of Mendocino, and is generally warmer than both. Cabernet and Zinfandel do best here. Some of the grapes go to Fetzer and other winemakers outside the county, but there are a few wineries (notably Guenoc) within the county.

The Central Coast

San Francisco Bay serves as an informal boundary between the North Coast and Central Coast, although the vineyards of Alameda and Santa Clara counties might fall in either classification. Wente and Concannon are the two major wineries in the Livermore Valley of Alameda County, a place long known for its Sauvignon Blanc and Semillon wines. Santa Clara County vineyard acreage has long been in decline, as houses and silicon chips have proven more profitable cash crops than grapes. Mirassou, J. Lohr, and Almaden wineries are located within the city limits of San Jose, but their vineyards are mostly farther south in Monterey and San Benito counties. Weibel has its sparkling-wine operation in Mission San Jose, but most of its wines are made in Mendocino County.

The Santa Cruz Mountains, backbone of the San Francisco peninsula, contain a number of small wineries in Santa Clara and Santa Cruz counties. Ridge, Mount Eden, Felton-Empire, and David Bruce are among the best known; all make wines from both the local grapes and those grown in other California locations. The Saratoga area used to be home to Paul Masson, but that winery has moved south to Monterey.

As early as 1935, researchers at the University of California at Davis identified Monterey County, specifically the Salinas Valley, as having

potential as a fine wine district. It was not until the 1960s, however, that significant acreage was planted. Monterey is now one of the largest producers of grapes and, increasingly, of wines, in the state. The northern end of the valley, around the town of Gonzales, is Region I; Soledad and Greenfield, Region II; and the upper valley above King City, Region III. Because this area was never planted with the vine before, growers gambled on finding (and keeping) it free of the vine parasite phylloxera (see page 8). As a result, vines in many Monterey vineyards are planted on their own rootstocks rather than grafted. So far, the experiment seems to be a success.

Ungrafted vines may be part of the reason for the characteristic intensity of fruit in Monterey wines. This intensity was not always considered a benefit; in the 1970s, Monterey wines were widely criticized for a strong herbaceous aroma sometimes described as "bell-pepper" and, less flatteringly, as "the Monterey veggies." As the young vines have matured and winemakers have gained experience with Monterey fruit, most wineries have learned to tame this quality, but the wines are still notable for the intensity of their varietal character. Riesling, Gewürztraminer, Chardonnay, Pinot Blanc, Gamay, Cabernet, and Pinot Noir are among the leading varieties. Paul Masson, Wente, San Martin, and Mirassou now rely largely on Monterey fruit. Jekel and Ventana are among the best of the smaller Monterey wineries.

San Benito County is similar to the warmer parts of Monterey County and has experienced a similar growth. It is perhaps a little better suited to red wines than Monterey County is; Almaden makes its best reds at its La Cienega and Paicines facilities.

The Gavilan mountain range, which separates the Salinas and San Benito valleys, contains an element

rare in California: limestone soil, one of the factors that adds to the quality of French Burgundies. One outcropping on the west is the Chalone Bench, a spot first planted with Pinot Noir, Chardonnay, and Pinot Blanc grapes in the last century. Many people consider Chalone wines the closest that California produces to the great red and white Burgundies of France. About ten miles north, an old limestone quarry on the San Benito side is the site of Calera, another fine producer of Burgundian Pinot Noir.

Another pioneering wine area lies to the west of the Salinas Valley. The upper Carmel Valley, inland from Big Sur in the Santa Lucia Mountains, is the site of much recent planting. Durney has shown the way with its award-winning Cabernet, and other Carmel Valley wines will be coming on the market in coming years.

San Luis Obispo County contains some of the oldest producing vineyards in the state, and some of the newest. Ridge Vineyards makes excellent Zinfandel from old vineyards near Paso Robles. (The newly recognized Paso Robles viticultural area is also one of the leaders in recent planting.) Estrella River is the most successful of the new wineries in the northern part of the county. Farther south, near the town of San Luis Obispo, the cool Region I climate of Edna Valley is fast becoming known for fine Chardonnay and other cool-season varieties.

A little farther south, the Santa Maria area of northern Santa Barbara County offers a similar ocean-cooled atmosphere. The extensive new plantings here are dominated by the large Tepusquet Vineyard, whose grapes have gone into a number of successful wines. Inland, but still cooled by ocean air, lies the Santa Ynez Valley, home of a number of wineries, including Firestone, Sanford, and Zaca Mesa. Firestone makes only estate-bottled Santa Ynez Valley wines, while Sanford blends wines from different sources, often under the "Central Coast" appellation.

The South Coast

Wine-growing south of the Tehachapi Mountains used to be limited to the Cucamonga area east of Los Angeles, but this area is now in decline due to urban sprawl. The leading Southern California vineyards are now located in San Diego County and the nearby Rancho California area of Riverside County. Callaway of Temecula was the pioneer in this area, planting vineyards in a few favored places where altitude and ocean air tempered the near-desert heat. They now market a very successful line of white wines. Culbertson specializes in San Diego County sparkling wines, including an excellent brut. San Pasqual is about to add sparkling wines to its line of table wines.

The Central Valley

The warm, fertile San Joaquin Valley contains the largest acreage of vineyards in the state. Most of it is Regions IV and V—ideal for table grapes, raisins, or dessert wines, but far too warm to make fine varietal wines. What the valley does produce is the best *vin ordinaire* in the world. Continuing research at the University of California at Davis, in the vineyards, and in the wineries has steadily improved the quality of San Joaquin Valley wines, and the trend will no doubt continue.

E. & J. Gallo of Modesto is the world's largest winery and the one that has introduced more Americans to table wine than any other. Gallo produces every conceivable type of wine—jug "burgundy" and "chablis," bulk-process "champagne," and a whole range of fortified, fruit-based, and flavored wines, as well as vintage-dated varietals, chiefly from the coastal counties. (Gallo is the single largest buyer of Napa Valley grapes, and a major buyer in Sonoma and Monterey counties as well.) The winery is also widely credited in the industry with introducing a whole generation of Americans to wine through their semisparkling "pop" wines; many a buyer of fine Chardonnay or Cabernet in the 1980s started with Boone's Farm or Ripple in the late 1960s.

Other giants of the valley include Guild, which makes the Cribari brand, Giumarra, and Franzia. Together, the valley wineries produce the majority of American wines.

There are, of course, smaller valley wineries. Some, like Ficklin and Quady, specialize in dessert wines. Others produce varietal table wines, particularly from Zinfandel grapes grown in the Lodi area and Chenin Blanc from the Clarksburg area of the Sacramento–San Joaquin Delta.

The Sierra Foothills

The lower foothills of the Sierra Nevada were first planted with vines shortly after the Gold Rush, and foothill vineyards have supplied grapes (especially Zinfandel) to wineries throughout the state for years. More recent plantings have brought renewed attention to this region. Roughly 1,000 to 3,000 feet in elevation, the vineyards of Amador, El Dorado, and Calaveras counties are somewhat cooler than the valley floor, mostly Region III and cooler Region IV. The older vines, especially, produce intense, ripe fruit in these areas, a fact that has prompted wineries such as Ridge and Sutter Home to buy grapes from Amador County and truck them back to their home bases in Cupertino and St. Helena. Even younger vines produce generous, fruity wines. Monteviña (founded 1973) was one of the first new foothill wineries making wines from old Amador County vineyards as well as new vines. Karly, Boeger, and Stevenot are among the more recent new wineries in the area. Zinfandel is still the leading variety, but newer vineyards also feature Cabernet, Sauvignon Blanc, and Chenin Blanc.

THE PACIFIC NORTHWEST

It is only a matter of geographic convenience to speak of the Pacific Northwest as one wine region, for it encompasses two completely different climates and numerous microclimates. The most important division is east to west, between the semiarid Columbia River basin east of the Cascade Range and the humid coastal belt west of the Cascades. So far, most Washington vineyards are on the east side and those of Oregon on the west, but future plantings on both sides in both states will probably soon confound the situation.

Insofar as it is possible to generalize about Northwest wines, they are lighter, higher in acid, and lower in alcohol than California wines. As a result, they have been called more "European" in style, a claim that has some validity. There are, of course, exceptions, including wines that taste quite Californian in style, but as a group, Northwest wines offer an alternative in flavor to California wines of the same varieties.

Eastern Washington

Washington winemakers make a big point of the fact that their vineyards lie at about the same latitude as the great wine regions of France. True enough, but the climates of the two places are not at all similar.

In fact, the conditions in eastern Washington are more or less unique: drier than anywhere in Europe or the eastern United States, cooler in summer than California (mostly Region I and II on the Davis heat-summation scale), milder in winter than New York State or the rest of the Northeast. The latitude comparison to Europe is valid in one respect: The longer summer days of the higher latitudes allow more ripening than areas of similar temperature farther south. Varieties that might not ripen fully in California Region I vineyards generally do fine in eastern Washington, even though the heat-summation figures are the same.

The major problem in this area is that winter temperatures can drop to the point of severe damage to all but the hardiest vines, but growers are learning how to protect their vines by partially burying the dormant vines and by controlling the irrigation of new plantings to encourage the roots to go deeper into the soil.

Another "problem" is that the extremely fertile soil of the Columbia Basin can cause vines to bear too heavily. Unless the grower controls this tendency, the vines can produce huge crops with widely varying sugar and acid levels. Here too, growers are learning how to deal with the unique conditions and produce the optimum amount of fruit per acre.

Washington has had a major grape industry since the 1860s, but until recently it was dominated by Concord and other labrusca varieties. In the last two decades, so many acres of vinifera vineyards have been planted in the eastern half of the state that Washington is now second only to California in total grape production and production of vinifera grapes and vinifera wines. (New York still produces more wine than Washington, but much of it is from out-of-state grapes.)

Most vinifera varieties have been tried in eastern Washington, but the most widely planted are White (Johannisberg) Riesling, Sauvignon Blanc, Semillon, Chenin Blanc, Chardonnay, Muscat Blanc, Gewürztraminer, Cabernet Sauvignon, Merlot, and Pinot Noir. So far Riesling has been the star variety among the whites, but Semillon, Chardonnay, and Gewürztraminer also do quite well here. Cabernets from this area can be excellent. They are generally a bit lighter and higher in acid than California Cabernets; it could be argued that these qualities make them better accompaniments to food. Merlot also shows good potential here. Pinot Noir has so far been less successful.

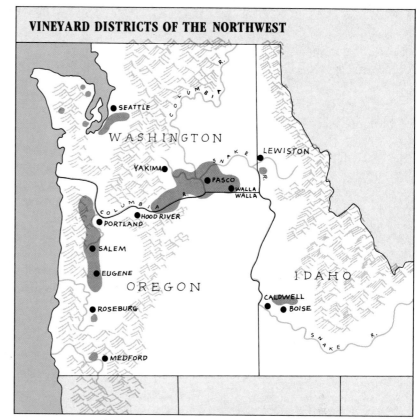

VINEYARD DISTRICTS OF THE NORTHWEST

Most of the plantings in eastern Washington are in the Yakima Valley, and that name is sometimes used to cover the whole region. But the Yakima Valley now has official status as a viticultural area and has defined boundaries. The other viticultural areas are the Walla Walla Valley and Columbia Valley, both of which include adjacent regions of Oregon. Plantings in the whole Columbia Basin are likely to increase.

Not all of the grapes grown in eastern Washington are crushed there. The Northwest's largest winery, Chateau Ste. Michelle, used to haul all its grapes over the Cascades to its original winery in the Seattle suburb of Woodinville before it opened two new facilities closer to the vineyards. Associated Vintners, another large winery, makes wines—mainly from eastern Washington grapes—in Bellevue, another Seattle suburb. And a number of Oregon wineries buy Washington grapes of varieties that are not suited to the cooler, moister regions of western Oregon.

Western Washington

The western third of Washington is as cool and rainy as the eastern part is sunny and dry. The conventional wisdom is that vinifera varieties will not ripen reliably here, but a handful of wineries in the Puget Sound area, led by Mount Baker Vineyards, are making good wines. The popular varieties are Gewürztraminer, Chardonnay, Müller-Thurgau (a German hybrid of Riesling and Sylvaner), a few French hybrids, and a number of unfamiliar varieties, including Madeline Angevine, Precoce de Malingre, and Okanogan Riesling. The last is described by Mount Baker as "a Hungarian hybrid of unknown heritage, with definite Riesling characteristics." It takes its name from the Okanogan Valley in British Columbia, where it is also grown.

The extreme southwest corner of Washington is close enough and similar enough to the Willamette Valley in Oregon that the following remarks about Oregon wines apply equally to the wines of Salishan Vineyards, located a half hour's drive north of Portland.

Western Oregon

Oregon's wine industry is much smaller than that of Washington, but it produces at least as many good wines. Aside from the small plantings in the Columbia Basin in the northeastern part of the state, Oregon's wine country is closer to the coast in the Willamette, Tualatin, Rogue, and Umpqua River valleys. Here the summers are cooler, the winters milder, and the weather quite a bit wetter than farther inland. Chardonnay, Riesling, and Gewürztraminer do well here, but the most exciting wine in Oregon is Pinot Noir.

Pinot Noir exemplifies the quality potential as well as the problems of the Oregon wine industry. The long, cool growing season is perfect for this grape, allowing it to develop an aroma and flavor that is more like French red Burgundy than Pinot Noir grown in California or Washington. In fact, as in Burgundy, many years are cool enough that the fully ripe-tasting grapes might contain only enough sugar to make wines of 7 or 8 percent alcohol. At these levels, the fermenting wine will not extract enough color or flavor from the grapes to make a commercially acceptable wine, so it is common (and fully legal) in Oregon to add sugar to the must. This practice, called *chaptalisation* in France, is widespread in Burgundy, in Germany, and in other cool areas of Europe. It is perfectly sound winemaking technique in cooler regions, although it is inappropriate in warmer areas like California.

Grapes are a tricky crop in Oregon. The higher humidity during the growing season requires careful control of fungus diseases. Sugar and acid levels and ripening patterns cannot be judged by the standards of other states. Also, because the harvest occurs later than in other regions, it coincides with the major fall migration of songbirds along the Pacific Flyway. A hungry flock of migrating robins can put a large dent in the

year's crop. Growers use a variety of techniques to repel birds, including noisemakers, nylon netting over the vines, and a chemical spray that tastes awful to the birds (but disappears in the winemaking process).

The reason growers and winemakers go to all this trouble is that when it works, the wines are excellent. The best Oregon wines have plenty of fruit, but in a more delicate (more "European") style than most California wines. Comparisons are unavoidable, but perhaps it is better to approach these wines without any preconceptions. In fact, it is a mistake to judge the wines of any region by the standards of another.

The farther south you go in western Oregon, the warmer and drier the climate becomes. Beginning around Roseburg in the Umpqua Valley, Cabernet and Merlot will ripen successfully along with the varieties that thrive farther north. Hillcrest, the oldest winery in the area, does quite well with both red and white wines. Look for more wines from southwestern Oregon in the years to come.

As a part of their quest for quality and consumer acceptance, Oregon winemakers have imposed on themselves the strictest labeling laws in the country. Varietal labels require at least 90 percent of the wine to be from the named variety, as opposed to 75 percent under federal law. Oregon also does not allow semi-generic names such as Burgundy; blended wines generally carry a proprietary name, such as Hinman Vineyards' "Tior," a white table wine.

Idaho

The lower elevations of Idaho are similar in climate to the Columbia Basin. Ste. Chapelle, built in the late 1970s, was the pioneering modern winery in this region. It has put Idaho on the wine map with its Chardonnay and Pinot Noir, and is now in major production of sparkling wines as well. Other new wineries in Idaho include Facelli, Weston, and Pucci.

NEW YORK

Until a few years ago, when it was passed by Washington, New York was the second biggest producer of wine grapes. (It still holds second place in volume of wine produced, but a substantial amount of the wine made in the state is from grapes grown elsewhere, including California.) New York remains the dominant winemaking state east of the Rockies.

Most winegrowing in New York is concentrated in the Finger Lakes region and the Lake Erie shore, both in the western half of the state. The Hudson Valley has a growing number of vineyards and wineries, and the tip of Long Island is beginning to show potential as well. What all of these areas have in common is proximity to large bodies of water, which moderate the extreme winter temperatures. Seneca Lake in the Finger Lakes, for example, has not frozen over since 1904. The mass of water in the lake absorbs heat all summer, then radiates it all winter, keeping the surrounding area warmer than the rest of the state, even during the coldest winters.

New York is a major battleground between proponents of French-American hybrids and vinifera grapes (see "The Hybrid Revolution in the East," page 11). The state's wine industry was formerly based on the hardy native American vine *Vitis labrusca,* but in the last few decades the hybrids have become the dominant type. Vinifera varieties, which have always had a small place in the New York wine industry, are now on the increase. Proponents of the hybrids say they are more reliable producers than viniferas and are better able to withstand the coldest winters. Advocates of vinifera say that the best hybrids are still no match for the choice vinifera varieties. So far, consumers have been willing to pay a premium for vinifera wines, making them worth the extra work and risk. The two types will most likely coexist for the foreseeable future in New York, and many wineries are adopting the sensible approach of making both hybrid and vinifera wines.

The Finger Lakes region is home to dozens of small wineries as well as the largest winery in the country outside California. The area around Keuka Lake is a good example of the diversity of the Finger Lakes. Taylor, in Hammondsport at the south end of the lake, is the giant of the eastern wine industry, the leading producer of New York "champagne" (under the Taylor and Great Western labels) as well as a full line of table and dessert wines. A few miles north lies Bully Hill, founded in 1970 by a disgruntled member of the Taylor family; it makes wines exclusively from hybrid grapes. Bully Hill varietals, such as Seyval Blanc, Cayuga, and Chancellor, and proprietary blends like "Old Church Red" and "Sweet Walter" are good examples of their types.

A little farther north on the west side of Keuka Lake is the vineyard and winery founded by Dr. Konstantin Frank. The appropriately named Vinifera Wine Cellars was the first Finger Lakes winery based entirely on European vinifera varieties—Riesling, Gewürztraminer, Pinot Noir, and Chardonnay. Beginning in the early 1960s, Dr. Frank proved that vinifera vines could not only survive in the Finger Lakes, but could make outstanding wines. Under the direction of his son Willy, the winery continues as the standard-bearer for vinifera wines in this region.

Nearby Heron Hill winery is typical of the newer Finger Lakes wineries, a small operation making both hybrid and vinifera wines. Their

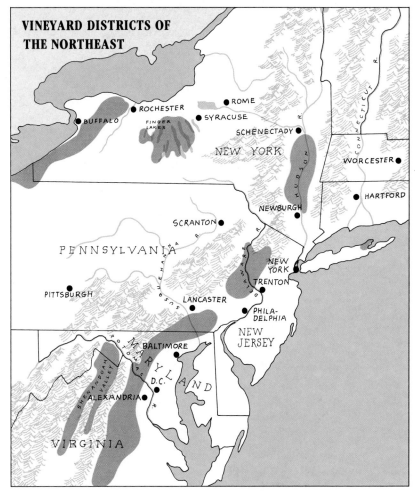

VINEYARD DISTRICTS OF THE NORTHEAST

Chardonnay and Riesling are well regarded, and they make an outstanding semisweet Vignoles under their second label, Otter Spring. At the north end of the lake, Chateau Esperanza is another producer of both hybrids and viniferas, including a Sauvignon Blanc—light and tart, perhaps, by California standards, but unmistakably varietal in character. Over on the eastern side of the lake, McGregor Vineyard produces mainly vinifera wines, including excellent late-harvest Riesling and Gewürztraminer that can stand with any made in the country. Other fine Finger

Lakes wineries include Glenora, which produces only white wines, Hermann Wiemer (vinifera only), Wickham, J. LeBeck, Plane's Cayuga Vineyard, and Frontenac Point.

Another major New York grape-growing district is along the shores of Lake Erie. Much of the production here is of Concord and other native grapes (this is the home of Mogen David kosher wines), but an increasing amount of hybrid grapes are being grown. Johnson Estate makes a good Chancellor as well as a number of hybrid whites. At the other end of the state, the Hudson Valley has a growing number of small wineries, including Benmarl, Cagnasso, Cascade Mountain, Cottage Vineyards, and Valley Vineyards.

New York's newest (and perhaps most promising) vineyard district is near the tip of Long Island. Hargrave Vineyard, near Cutchogue on the North Fork, was the pioneer in this area, planting Chardonnay, Cabernet Sauvignon, and other viniferas in the mid-1970s. Hargrave Cabernet is a fine, well-balanced wine, fairly early to mature (the 1981 was quite drinkable in early 1985). Other vineyards, including Bridgehampton and Lenz, have followed in the area, and there are probably more in the works.

THE MID-ATLANTIC STATES

Vinifera vineyards were first planted in Virginia by Lord Delaware in 1619, but it is only in this century that they have become commercially feasible. Today, the Piedmont area of northern Virginia, western Maryland, and southern Pennsylvania, lying on the eastern foothills of the Appalachian range, is among the fastest-growing wine regions of the country.

Like other eastern states, Virginia and Maryland grow a combination of hybrid and vinifera grapes. Philip Wagner first introduced the hybrids in his Boordy Vineyards near Baltimore, and still operates a nursery there, having retired from the winemaking part of the operation. Hybrids are generally more reliable, being better adapted to the humid summers and the fungus diseases endemic to the region. But many growers are learning how to grow viniferas as well. (As in New York and other eastern states, vinifera wines attract more attention and command higher prices, making them commercially attractive.) Both types will likely have a place in the future of the mid-Atlantic wine industry.

Among the best producers of Virginia wines are Meredyth, Ingleside Plantation, Montdomaine Cellars (under the Monticello Wine Co. label), and Farfelu. In Maryland, in addition to Boordy, there are Montbray, which has received high praise for its Cabernet, and several newer wineries.

West Virginia and Pennsylvania also have small but growing wine industries, although their development was held back for many years by high state license fees for wineries. Some experts suggest that there may be Piedmont locations as far south as Georgia where wine grapes will do well. The southeastern Coastal Plain has so far proven inhospitable to wine grapes; only the native Muscadine grapes, a large-fruited type only distantly related to most other grapes, can survive the high summer humidity and native vine diseases here. Muscadines make a distinctive, very fragrant type of wine, usually sweetened and sold under the name Scuppernong.

THE GREAT LAKES STATES AND THE MIDWEST

The grape-growing belt along the southern shore of Lake Erie that begins in New York extends through part of Pennsylvania and across northern Ohio and into southeastern Michigan. Ohio was once the largest wine-producing state in the country, and still produces a lot of wine. Native labrusca grapes are still common, but hybrids and viniferas are on the increase. Isle St. George, one of a cluster of islands in Lake Erie, has its own viticultural-area appellation, and has recently seen major plantings of vinifera varieties.

Michigan's vineyards are also mostly located near water. The southwest corner of the state along Lake Michigan produces both table and wine grapes, and has several wineries, of which Tabor Hill is the best known. Farther north, the Leelanau Peninsula is the site of major recent plantings, mostly of hybrids. Boskydel Vineyard and L. Mawby are the leading names in this newly recognized viticultural area.

A number of new vineyards and wineries have appeared in the Ohio Valley (southern Ohio, Indiana, and Illinois, and northern Kentucky) in the last decade or so. Missouri has a long history of winemaking, mostly based on labrusca varieties, around the town of Hermann. Newer wineries in the state are making mostly hybrid wines. A fair amount of wine is also made in the Ozark Plateau of Arkansas, mostly by the Wiederkehr and Post wineries.

THE SOUTHWEST

Texas is on the verge of being a major winemaking state. There are several new vinifera vineyards and wineries in the central Texas hill country, and large new plantings in the western part of the state as well as New Mexico and Arizona. The higher elevations in the mountains are cool enough to compare with some of the coastal counties of California and are being planted with choice varietals; the lowlands are generally being planted to the same bulk varieties as are grown in the climatically similar San Joaquin Valley. Tens of thousands of acres of vineyards are either planted or in the works across the Southwest, many of them funded by European interests. The area shows some promise of quality wines, but the sheer volume of the new plantings leads some industry observers to wonder who will drink all the wine they produce.

INDEX

Note: Page numbers in italics refer to illustrations separated from recipe text.

U.S. MEASURE AND METRIC MEASURE CONVERSION CHART

		Formulas for Exact Measures			Rounded Measures for Quick Reference		
	Symbol	When you know:	Multiply by	To find:			
Mass (Weight)	oz	ounces	28.35	grams	1 oz		= 30 g
	lb	pounds	0.45	kilograms	4 oz		= 115 g
	g	grams	0.035	ounces	8 oz		= 225 g
	kg	kilograms	2.2	pounds	16 oz	= 1 lb	= 450 g
					32 oz	= 2 lb	= 900 g
					36 oz	= 2¼ lb	= 1,000 g (1 kg)
Volume	tsp	teaspoons	5.0	milliliters	¼ tsp	= ¹⁄₂₄ oz	= 1 ml
	tbsp	tablespoons	15.0	milliliters	½ tsp	= ¹⁄₁₂ oz	= 2 ml
	fl oz	fluid ounces	29.57	milliliters	1 tsp	= ⅙ oz	= 5 ml
	c	cups	0.24	liters	1 tbsp	= ½ oz	= 15 ml
	pt	pints	0.47	liters	1 c	= 8 oz	= 250 ml
	qt	quarts	0.95	liters	2 c (1 pt)	= 16 oz	= 500 ml
	gal	gallons	3.785	liters	4 c (1 qt)	= 32 oz	= 1 l.
	ml	milliliters	0.034	fluid ounces	4 qt (1 gal)	= 128 oz	= 3¾ l.
Length	in.	inches	2.54	centimeters	⅜ in.		= 1 cm
	ft	feet	30.48	centimeters	1 in.		= 2.5 cm
	yd	yards	0.9144	meters	2 in.		= 5 cm
	mi	miles	1.609	kilometers	2½ in.		= 6.5 cm
	km	kilometers	0.621	miles	12 in. (1 ft)		= 30 cm
	m	meters	1.094	yards	1 yd		= 90 cm
	cm	centimeters	0.39	inches	100 ft		= 30 m
					1 mi		= 1.6 km
Temperature	° F	Fahrenheit	⅝ (after subtracting 32)	Celsius	32° F		= 0° C
					68 °F		= 20° C
	° C	Celsius	⅝ (then add 32)	Fahrenheit	212° F		= 100° C
Area	in.²	square inches	6.452	square centimeters	1 in.²		= 6.5 cm²
	ft²	square feet	929.0	square centimeters	1 ft²		= 930 cm²
	yd²	square yards	8,361.0	square centimeters	1 yd²		= 8,360 cm²
	a	acres	0.4047	hectares	1 a		= 4,050 m²

Special Thanks to:

David Adelsheim, Newberg, OR
Carole Basso, San Francisco, CA
Laura Bishop, Ithaca, NY
Barbara Chambers, San Francisco, CA
Mr. and Mrs. Charles Crocker,
  San Francisco, CA
Willy Frank, Hammondsport, NY
Richard H. Graff, San Francisco, CA
David Lett, Dundee, OR
Bill Nelson, Roseburg, OR
Elaine Ratner, Oakland, CA
San Francisco International Cheese
  Imports, Inc., San Francisco, CA
Archie Smith, Jr., and Archie Smith III,
  Middleburg, VA
Philip Wagner, Riderwood, MD
John Walker and Co. Liquors,
  San Francisco, CA
The Wine Institute, San Francisco, CA

**Thanks to the following wineries
for their help and cooperation in
the preparation of this book:**

CALIFORNIA

Acacia Winery, Napa
Adelaida Cellars, Paso Robles
Alexander Valley Vineyards, Healdsburg
Almaden Vineyards, San Jose
Amador Foothill Winery, Plymouth
Bargetto's Santa Cruz Winery, Soquel
Beaulieu Vineyard, Rutherford
Belvedere Winery, Healdsburg
Beringer Vineyards, St. Helena
Bouchaine Vineyards, Napa
Buehler Vineyards, St. Helena
Buena Vista Winery and Vineyards,
  Sonoma
Burgess Cellars, St. Helena
Carmenet Vineyard, Sonoma
Carneros Creek Winery, Napa
Chalone Vineyard, Soledad
Chateau St. Jean, Inc., Kenwood
The Christian Brothers, Napa
Clos du Bois, Healdsburg
Conn Creek Winery, St. Helena
R. & J. Cook, Clarksburg
Deloach Vineyards, Santa Rosa
Devlin Wine Cellars, Soquel
Domaine Laurier Winery & Vineyards,
  Forestville

Durney Vineyard, Carmel Valley
Edna Valley Vineyard, San Luis Obispo
Estrella River Winery, Paso Robles
Far Niente Winery, Oakville
The Firestone Vineyard, Los Olivos
L. Foppiano Wine Co., Healdsburg
Frick Winery, Santa Cruz
E. & J. Gallo Winery, Modesto
Gibson Wine Co., Sanger
Girard Winery, Oakville
Glen Ellen Winery, Glen Ellen
Grand Cru Vineyards, Glen Ellen
Groth Vineyards & Winery, Oakville
Guenoc Winery, Middletown
Gundlach-Bundschu Winery, Vineburg
Hacienda Wine Cellars, Sonoma
Heitz Wine Cellars, St. Helena
William Hill Winery, Napa
HMR Ltd., Paso Robles
Inglenook Vineyards, Rutherford
Italian Swiss Colony, Asti
Jekel Vineyard, Greenfield
Jordan Vineyard & Winery, Healdsburg
Robert Keenan Winery, St. Helena
Kathryn Kennedy Winery, Saratoga
Kenwood Vineyards, Kenwood
Charles Krug Winery, St. Helena
Landmark Vineyards, Windsor
Lolonis Winery, Redwood Valley
Lower Lake Winery, Lower Lake
M. Marion & Co., Saratoga
Mark West Vineyards, Forestville
Martin Brothers, Paso Robles
Louis M. Martini, St. Helena
Paul Masson Vineyards, Saratoga
Matanzas Creek Winery, Santa Rosa
Mirassou Vineyards, San Jose
Robert Mondavi Winery, Oakville
R. Montali Winery, Berkeley
Monterey Peninsula Winery, Monterey
The Monterey Vineyard, Gonzales
Monticello Cellars, Napa
Mountain House Winery, Cloverdale
Robert Pecota Winery, Calistoga
J. Pedroncelli Winery, Geyserville
Joseph Phelps Vineyards, St. Helena
Quady Winery, Madera
Ridge Vineyards & Winery, Cupertino
Rutherford Hill Winery, Rutherford
Saintsbury, Napa
Sanford Winery, Buellton
Sea Ridge Winery, Cazadero
Sebastiani Vineyards, Sonoma
Sequoia Grove Vineyards, Napa
Shafer Vineyards, Napa

Charles F. Shaw Vineyard & Winery,
  St. Helena
Silver Oak Wine Cellars, Oakville
Silverado Vineyards, Napa
Simi Winery, Healdsburg
Smith & Hook Winery, Gonzales
Spring Mountain Vineyards, St. Helena
Sterling Vineyards, Calistoga
Stevenot Winery, Murphys
Topolos at Russian River, Forestville
Trefethen Vineyards, Napa
Turgeon-Lohr Winery, San Jose
Vichon Winery, Oakville
Villa Mt. Eden Winery, Oakville
Weibel Champagne Vineyards,
  Mission San Jose
Zaca Mesa Winery, Los Olivos
ZD Wines, Napa

NEW YORK

Bully Hill, Hammondsport
Glenora Wine Cellars, Dundee
Heron Hill Vineyards, Hammondsport
Long Island Vineyards, Cutchogue
McGregor Vineyard, Dundee
The Taylor Wine Co., Hammondsport
Hermann J. Wiemer Vineyard, Dundee
Vinifera Wine Cellars, Hammondsport

OREGON

Adelsheim Vineyard, Newberg
Amity Vineyards, Amity
Chateau Benoit, Carlton
Ellendale Vineyards, Dallas
The Eyrie Vineyards, Dundee
Hillcrest Vineyard, Roseburg
Hinman Vineyards, Eugene

VIRGINIA

Ingleside Plantation Vineyards, Oak Grove
Meredyth Vineyard, Middleburg
Montdomaine Cellars, Charlottesville

WASHINGTON

Arbor Crest/Washington Cellars, Spokane
Associated Vintners, Bellevue
Champs de Brionne Winery, Quincy
Chateau Ste. Michelle Vintners,
  Woodinville
Hoodsport Winery, Hoodsport
Mount Baker Vineyards, Everson
Tucker Cellars, Sunnyside
Yakima River Winery, Prosser